Come Back To Waiʻoli

Come Back To

Wai'oli

A Brief History of
The Salvation Army
Wai'oli Tea Room
Manoa Valley ~ Honolulu Hawaii

By Bette McAbee-Vincent Stillwell

Published by
Bette McAbee~Vincent Stillwell

Art Direction & Design by
Viki Nasu Design Group

Library of Congress
Catalog Card Number: 99-90374
ISBN 0-9674829-0-9

Second Printing June 2004

Stillwell, Bette McAbee~Vincent, 1999
Come Back to Wai'oli:
A Brief History of
The Salvation Army Wai'oli Tea Room
Manoa Valley • Honolulu, Hawaii
(alk. Paper)

Printed in China

*T*his book is dedicated
to the Salvation Army
officers and workers who gave
so unselfishly, the best of their
ability in the cause of "others."

Every effort has been made to
authenticate names and dates
and the writer apologizes for
any parts of the history that
may have been missed.

*In loving memory of
Commandant Clara M. Long
and Staff Captain Libbie McAbee
for their devotion to God
and their pioneer efforts
in establishing
The Salvation Army
Children's Home on this site.*

TABLE OF CONTENTS

Section II • Bette's Story 1978–1999

PREFACE

ommencing in 1980, documented information for this writing has come through correspondence with Salvation Army personnel whose service included involvement with The Wai'oli Tea Room, personal interviews, and extensive research through files, books, and publications containing pertinent historical detail.

It is intended to serve as a record of history from the beginning of The Salvation Army's renowned Girls' Home in 1909, later known as the Children's Home, and later still, The Salvation Army Residential Treatment Facilities for Children. It goes on through the continuing saga of a historic architectural and gastronomical establishment in a lush residential area in the city of Honolulu. For anyone who lived there as a child or served there as a worker, it holds unforgettable memories.

ACKNOWLEDGEMENTS

The person who first interested me in documenting the history of the Wai'oli Tea Room was Elsie Monma, a devoted member of its staff for almost thirty years. As assistant manager, she "ran" the Gift Shop. Day after day she responded to queries about the Tea Room's origin, admonishing me to write a book that could answer all the questions. The late Brigadier Sara Jones was another key figure who inspired me with volumes of hand-written memoirs that she shared over a period of fifteen years. Lt.Colonel Muriel Mitchell Collier, retired Salvation Army officer and former head of the Girls' Home, added warmth and personality to the many characters who comprised the ever-changing Wai'oli Tea Room community during the course of 90 years.

The Tea Room would not have been created without the presence and commitment of The Salvation Army; the hundreds of staff officers who dedicated their lives to the service of God and the care and keeping of others, especially children, in Hawaii. Their consistent image of charity to all has been matched with essential financial support from the community at large.

I wish to thank my three editors: Mary M. Cooke, Kenneth R. Harding, and Dorry Wollstein for their most qualified help. The entire project was moved along with the constant encouragement and advice of my husband of fifty years, Dr. Robert J. Stillwell.

INTRODUCTION

I fell in love with the Wai'oli Tea Room many years ago. It was 1966 when, with four teenaged sons, my husband and I arrived as Salvation Army officers in Honolulu. We were assigned to work with boys and girls in the care of The Salvation Army Residential Treatment Facilities for Children on two campuses; Manoa and Diamond Head (Kaimuki); my husband was the administrator. The Tea Room was on the Manoa property; originally an adjunct training center for children in residence with The Salvation Army Home. Our living quarters was close by, a historic old home owned by The Salvation Army.

As our time in Hawaii progressed I learned that the Children's Home and its surrounding ten acres along Manoa Road and Oahu Avenue had been acquired in 1909 under the leadership of missionary ancestors of my mother's family; two young Salvation Army officers who had been assigned to head "Rescue Home" work with neglected women and children in Honolulu. Theirs was not a singular accomplishment but old files and correspondence between their offices and some of Hawaii's most notable families attest to the fact that their aggressive labors to find money for The Salvation Army project were not in vain.

Construction of a three-story "cottage" was underway before the end of 1909. Staff-Captain Libby McAbee and Commandant Clara M. Long had accomplished their task, leaving a legacy that would grow and grow as Hawaii's children found refuge and love in this Salvation Army *ohana* (family).

A bronze plaque set on a stone rests permanently in their honor near the Wai'oli Chapel, given by Richard and Julia McAbee; Libby McAbee's nephew and Clara Long's adopted daughter.

Julia Pratae was a sickly two-year old child when she was placed in the Salvation Army's care in Honolulu. Clara Long cared for her in her own quarters until the child's health improved, and upon departing Hawaii in 1912, obtained formal adoption of the then six-year-old Julia. Clara Long was a single mother long before the practice became popular. Julia grew to womanhood and, with her mother, remained close to the McAbee family in Seattle, Washington. In 1926 Julia married F. Richard (Dick) McAbee, my mother's younger brother. Long-time residents of Seattle, Dick and Julia lived

1981: Dick and Julia McAbee at McAbee & Long marker near the Wai'oli Chapel.

well into their nineties. Mr. McAbee was a respected property developer and philanthropist as well as a life-member of The Salvation Army Advisory Board of Seattle.

Our residence while in Honolulu was at the top of Rainbow Drive in Manoa Valley. Built in 1928, the house was a gift from Mr. George N. Wilcox to the women who implemented the founding of the Wai'oli Tea Room; Commandant Rachel Payne and Adjutant Carrie Sabine. These two women were appointed by The Salvation Army to take on where McAbee and Long had left off in 1912.

No organization has done more to bring comfort to the needy or to bear witness to the love and teachings of Jesus Christ as laid forth in the Bible. "Come Back to Wai'oli" is the written record of a treasured place, where lives were impacted through love and example. This humble account is dedicated to the men and women of The Salvation Army who are known for their good works and whose faith in God is a testament for the ages. They made a difference in Hawaii.

WAI'OLI

1909~1978

IN THE BEGINNING

or seventy-five years visitors young and old have found their way back to the Wai'oli Tea Room, remembering a moment in time that continues to touch their soul with joy. Its original purpose served Hawaii's children as a vocational training adjunct to The Salvation Army's Children's Home established in Manoa Valley in 1909. Built on the site in 1922, it served as a "classroom" for nearly forty years. A simple but most unique presentation eventually

Artist rendering of Cooke Cottage 1909.

"put it on the map" as a treasured Afternoon Tea or luncheon destination. To this day countless visitors to Oahu seek and find the hideaway they remember from so long ago, the Manoa landmark; added to the State and National Registries of Historic Places in 1991. Over the years tour guides have filled the heads of eager visitors to Wai'oli with assorted tales of its origin, romance, and intrigue, most with scant resemblance to the true story.

As a matter of fact: The early years of the twentieth century in Hawaii's history were fraught with political and economic upheaval. Disease and infection often went unattended and it was not uncommon

Rescue Home Children & Staff 1908.

for women to die in childbirth. The Salvation Army was sought out soon after the organization's arrival in 1894 to rescue young women and children who were in dire need. The Children's Home (Girls' Home) in then remote Manoa Valley replaced a small single-family residence at 1680 South King Street, the first "Rescue Home" that by 1909 was too small.

Wai'oli's history involves hundreds of people; men and women, boys and girls whose lives were affected by even a short stay in this environment. The property was acquired in 1909 through the generosity of many prominent members of Hawaii's early missionary families including the Dillinghams, Athertons, Cookes, Isenbergs, and George N. Wilcox of Kauai. The first structure, Wilcox Cottage, was "a substantial, well built home of twenty-two rooms and dormitories with accommodations for fifty or more girls." The Cooke Cottage was added by that family in 1911; Dillingham Cottage in 1915 by Mother Baldwin, Mrs. Maude B. Cooke and G.N. Wilcox, and Hale Ola, "house of recovery" in 1919 by Mrs. Dora Isenberg and the Wilcox sisters, Elsie and Mabel. This detail was covered in a 1957 issue of *Paradise of the Pacific*, forerunner to *Honolulu Magazine*, by Ah Jook Ku, a writer for The Salvation Army at that time.

*1920's:
Commandant
Rachel Payne
(left) and Major
Carrie Sabine
(right) with
Girls' Home
String Band.*

There was a steady increase in the numbers of children coming into the home and by 1920, statistics show 100 children in residence in these four large cottages. More than half of the children were of high school age, and out of the need for practical vocational training, the Waiʻoli Tea Room came into being.

Commandant Rachel Payne and Adjutant Carrie Sabine had been appointed to head the Girls' Home, arriving from British Columbia in 1912. Tea rooms in Canada were a part of Payne and Sabine's culture and they were very familiar with what was involved in such an enterprise. They were pleased that the idea was accepted with much enthusiasm, knowing that a tea room could offer classes in cooking and baking, simple food preparation, serving, and cleanup along with exposure to the commercial community with the serving of Afternoon Tea.

The terms "Afternoon Tea" and "High Tea" are often confused. Today it appears that either is correct when referring to an afternoon repast, although each format has a specific origin. "High Tea" was the Victorian working man's last meal of the day; an early supper which allowed him to get to bed before dark. It also provided him with the sustenance needed to perform hard labor. A combination of hot dishes,

1927 photo of the Salvation Army Girls' Home in Manoa (l to r) Cooke Cottage, staff residence, Wilcox Cottage, the infirmary and (in far right corner) roof of Wai'oli Tea Room. Water sheds clung to the hillside.

chicken, game, or ham served with salads, breads, cheeses, and an endless assortment of cakes and condiments, this meal consisted of anything available in the pantry. For most, it was the bridge between a light lunch and a simple breakfast.

"Afternoon Tea" on the other hand, was generally a custom for higher society, whether that of the aristocracy or the prosperous middle and upper-middle classes. A delicate affair of scones and jam, cucumber finger sandwiches and tea cakes was served in the afternoon, long after lunch and several hours before dinner. ("*Tea Time*" by M. Dalton King, 1992. Running Press, Philadelphia • London.)

The Tea Room idea began to take shape and, once again, a major portion of the funds needed for construction and furnishings came from George Norton Wilcox, the generous friend from the Island of Kauai.

Honolulu architects, Emory and Webb, drew up the building plans in a style that would fit the residential neighborhood. The Arts and Crafts Movement of architecture – a "California Bungalow" design showed wide lanais and floor-to-ceiling window openings to accommodate life in humid Manoa Valley.

WAI'OLI'S FIRST DECADE

ormal dedication ceremonies in November of 1922 brought together elected Territorial officials, friends, Salvation Army staff and dignitaries from mainland America. The young people of the home were included in a special program and Afternoon Tea was served for the first time. With this introduction it didn't take long for the new Tea Room to "catch on" and within the first few years Wai'oli had become a popular daytime setting for the local gentry.

Wai'oli's kitchen and dining areas became the activity center of choice for many of the children and the training proved to be an excellent diversion from the traditional classroom format.

The first decade was filled with excitement including a stressful bout with the Chamber of Commerce and local small businesses accusing the Wai'oli Tea Room Bakery, run by a non-profit organization, of taking unfair advantage of the competition. After months of long dissertations between Salvation Army officials (then Divisional Commander Colonel C. Wilfred Bourne) and the Honolulu community, the problem was resolved. The bakery was allowed to continue to sell to the public but delivery to downtown hotel dining rooms and restaurants was halted. Despite this change, business flourished.

PHOTO: BISHOP MUSEUM

Wai'oli Girls' Home Bakery Wagon 1926.

(above) George N. Wilcox is pictured with young women of the Girls' Home on the new steps of the rebuilt "Robert Louis Stevenson Grass Shack at ceremonies dedicating the Grass Hut, 1926.

(left) Original newspaper clipping March 1926.

A House to Give Away

A monument to the "Good Old Days of the Monarchy," homeless, is awaiting a haven where it can rest a little longer, at least for sentiment's sake.

Who is there who has a little plot of vacant land to spare at Waikiki and will remove the famous old grass house which belonged to Princess Kaiulani, at Ainahau, to a place where its memories and associations will be preserved?

Our fellow-townsman, James W. Bergstrom, bought the lot at Ainahau some time back and has recently sold the portion where the old grass house stands, but the new owner has other plans in mind than to make his home in this famous old "Honeymoon Cottage," Mr. Bergstrom would like to know who wants it.

The grass house was built about sixty years ago. If its walls could speak there would be many a tale of the roystering times when Robert Louis Stevenson and his coterie of "hale fellows—well met," here drank and shouted their paeans of revelry. Merry monarchs, princes and plebians, men of the sea and men of war, youth eternal and wanderers of all climes, knew this spot.

It is a bit of the Old Hawaii that cannot be replaced. Who will give these mute grass walls a home?

1926 Original Grass Hut.

Rachel Payne was a born marketer. Her attention to customer service put her ahead of her time and Wai'oli's following grew quickly. A small newspaper article caught her eye one day in March of 1926 and obviously sparked her scheme to bring more visitors to the Tea Room. Within hours after seeing the article she had hired transportation and made her way with a driver and a flatbed wagon to Waikiki to make the first bid on a small grass shack that was being auctioned away. Her early arrival prompted the first bid and sure enough, it was accepted. The shack was dismantled piece by piece and along with the simple furnishings, was loaded onto the wagon. They must have made an interesting picture, this very dignified matron sitting with the young Hawaiian on the driver's seat and behind them a stack of assorted lengths and widths of boards, bundles of grass, a table and chairs, floor lamp and book shelf. The uphill course into Manoa Valley might have taken an hour and when the wagon was sighted entering the roadway into the property, a cheer of excitement could be heard from the welcoming workers and children. She had accomplished her mission, but what would she do with this wagonload of what looked like debris!

PHOTO: BISHOP MUSEUM

1925 Afternoon Tea on the Lanai. Waiʻoli Tea Room.

Rachel Payne knew exactly what she was going to do with it! Soon after the arrival of the wagon, a clearing was prepared in the garden just to the rear of the main building. Within a few days it was completed. A little grass shack, transplanted from Ainahau in Waikiki, the former property of the Princess Kaʻiulani and her parents, was now a visitor attraction to The Waiʻoli Tea Room. Just as it was planned! Legends surrounding the grass shack had run the gamut from romance to gardening and Rachel Payne named it "The Robert Louis Stevenson Grass Shack." That was 1926! It became the backdrop for picture taking by everyone who visited the Tea Room for more than a half century. Visitors had their own tales to tell as to the shack's history and perhaps that's exactly what Rachel Payne had in mind when she decided to put it to rest in Waiʻoli's garden.

1927 Tea in the Garden. Waiʻoli Tea Room.

A new wing was added to the Tea Room's main building in 1926 providing a sizeable increase in dining space. The room was designed with triple-hung windows seven feet high, that could be raised to allow complete open space. A huge stone fireplace was centered between the unique windows on the front wall. Stone balustrades with wrought iron railings extended beyond the window openings on the two-story front side of the building. A bay window on the rear wall made a perfect frame for the Robert Louis Stevenson Grass Shack. It was a beautiful addition.

A letter from G.N. Wilcox shared his regrets in not being able to attend the festive party that was held to celebrate the building completion.

Rachel Payne and Carrie Sabine retired in 1928 and moved into their new stone house high on the hillside behind the Tea Room buildings.

PHOTOS: SARA JONES

(above) "Kauai Room" interior of the new dining room added c. 1926.
(top) A glimpse through the arches—Wai‘oli Tea Room interior dining spaces, 1929.

THE THIRTIES

3

Lieutenant Sara Kennedy (Jones) sailed from San Francisco to Honolulu with her friend Lieutenant Julia Gerlach (Mollet) in July of 1929. Upon graduating from The Salvation Army's College for Officers these two young women were appointed to serve on the staff of The Salvation Army Girls' Home in Honolulu.

The freighter *Manoa* carried a hundred or more passengers, described by Sara as "lovely people." She said that after ten days at sea the excitement on deck was electric approaching the dock in Honolulu Harbor. The familiar sound of brass instruments was not a Salvation Army band but The Royal Hawaiian Band, that greeted all cruise ship arrivals. Sara described the bronze-skinned divers whose lithe bodies churned the clear waters scampering after coins dropping from the ship's decks above. Providing a colorful picture were many women dressed in bright colored *muumuus* laden with beautiful flower leis. Sara and Julia strained their eyes looking for a familiar face in the crowd below and before long they spotted the white hats and uniforms of Major Carolyn Antrim and members of the Girls' Home staff, who were doing the same, looking to greet them. As they set their feet on the dock, they were nearly smothered by leis and hugs and kisses on their cheeks. What a welcome it was! Their ride to Manoa Valley was a sightseeing tour through downtown Honolulu past beautiful parks and gardens along the way. Major Antrim, head of the Girls' Home at that time, told something of what they could expect in their new home in the first few days. Wai'oli Tea Room was part of the Girls' Home and it held a very important place in the care and education of many children.

Large two-story dwellings (cottages they called them) were named for benefactors: Dillingham Cottage housed the babies and the youngest

(above) Wilcox Cottage housed children ages 10–13. (right) Dillingham Cottage housed babies and the youngest children.

children, Cooke Cottage – ages 6 - 9, Wilcox Cottage ages 10 - 13, and the main building housed the older teenagers. Sara lived in the Wilcox building of two dormitories with 25 to 30 girls. They awoke at 5 A.M. and school started at 7 A.M. They worked twelve-hour days and fell into their beds just after nine o'clock at night.

Sara and Julia's days were filled with activities ranging from house-cleaning and food preparation to working with children's activities in the Tea Room. Windows and floors were polished every day. Fresh coconut had to be shredded everyday. Mango, papaya, guava and pineapple were peeled and chopped for use in the day's baking of jams and jelly, and fruit compotes for teatime. It wasn't long before they were adept at all of the tasks that made up the morning routine. Wai'oli's kitchen and other work areas served as daily classrooms providing an education unlike any other school.

In the early Thirties Captain Helena Sainsbury joined the Girls' Home staff and spent many afternoon hours hostessing tea parties at

1930's Wai'oli Tea Room Lanai Dining.   *Captain Helena Sainsbury*

Wai'oli. Helena was tall and slender, and in her crisp white uniform made a very attractive picture as she seated guests and moved among the tea tables. The older girls in the home were selected for the Afternoon Tea duty wearing cotton dresses of their own choosing. They set the tables, served the tea and delicacies, then washed the dishes. On checking the day's reservations, Captain Sainsbury recognized the name hosting a party of three for Afternoon Tea; Miss Kahanamoku was a sister of Duke Kahanamoku, the world-class swimmer and surfer. They arrived on time and Helena was taken aback noticing Miss Kahanamoku's guests to be Doris Duke Cromwell and her bodyguard, Marion; "a woman of size," as she put it. They were greeted enthusiastically and seated to their pleasure. Mrs. Cromwell was a well-known figure in Honolulu society and throughout the world. Her reputation preceded her as a very forthright woman with a demanding air.

A young lady served water as the ladies exchanged pleasantries, their eyes glancing around the dining room and surrounding gardens, with eyebrows raised in what appeared to be approval. Before leaving their table the waitress was held in conversation by Mrs. Cromwell who instructed her to add a shot of rum to the tea to aid her friend who was nursing a cold. Miss Sainsbury was summoned immediately to intercede for the young woman who did not know how to answer the wish of this

Dillingham Cottage "artisans" in rocking chairs.

lady. Helena approached the scene with a modicum of anxiety but quietly informed Mrs. Cromwell of The Salvation Army's stand on alcohol and added that no liquor was allowed on the premises. With no more than a shrug of her shoulders, conversation was resumed as they proceeded with their afternoon repast.

On another day a large luxury liner was in port. Miss Sainsbury had taken a call requesting afternoon tea for one hundred fifty guests for the next day. This number on one day, arriving simultaneously, was an unusually large order requiring the staff to work well into the evening in preparation of the volume of food that would be served. The dining rooms were set at capacity for tea service of this size.

The tables looked lovely, each with a simple vase of flowers. The buses arrived at the appointed time and guests were seated in an orderly manner, seeming to anticipate what was coming. As tea pots were being placed on each table, platters of dainty sandwiches, scones and jam, meat pastries, and sweet cakes were passed to guests around the tables.

Captain Sainsbury was transferred to serve on the staff of The Salvation Army Girls' Home in Hilo where she met and cared for thirty-six little girls and young women. She retired in Belfair, Washington.

Salvation Army Girls' Home Band, 1931. Brigadier Albert E. Baynton, Divisional Commander.

Teapots were refilled frequently and everyone appeared to be having a good time. As the hostess walked from table to table she distinguished five different languages being spoken. Wai'oli was truly an international setting.

The Gift Shop was always busy with customers buying jams and jellies packed in attractive *tapa* lined boxes for shipment around the world. Colored tissue paper protected the jars and on each was pinned a scenic postcard of Hawaii. There was no such convenience as transparent tape in those days.

With growing numbers of people finding their way to the Wai'oli Tea Room, bakery orders swelled, as did orders for the jams and jellies. Every day was a new adventure; new people, new experiences. It was the bakery that established Wai'oli's reputation with faithful customers. The holiday season prompted many special orders for fruitcakes of every size as well as Swedish/German Stollen breads and cookies wrapped for gift giving.

Wai'oli Children's Chapel situated at the foot of the tea room, was built in 1939. Most of its structure consists of native lava rock.

Throughout the Thirties, Wai'oli was a venerable establishment in the Manoa community. Despite depressed times throughout the world many people were cruising the high seas and Honolulu was an attractive port of call. The Wai'oli Tea Room had been discovered as a luncheon destination for large groups of visitors putting ashore for one day only, and on many Saturdays Wai'oli served as many as 300 visitors. Oven fried chicken was the order of the day and the luncheon included Coconut Cream Pie, all for $1.50. The flurry of a full house only increased Wai'oli's popularity.

The Children's Chapel, as it was called originally, was built in 1939 just across from the Tea Room main entrance. It was used for worship on Sundays and for Christian education at scheduled times throughout the week. Thick lava rock walls kept the interior temperature cooler than outside and long wooden pews were set opposite a wide center aisle. It was a beautiful edifice for worship and learning. Wai'oli enjoyed much good favor throughout the Thirties and it was apparent to everyone, whether visitor or local resident, that The Salvation Army was serving a great need in the lives of many young people in Honolulu.

4

THE WAR YEARS AND BEYOND

On December 7, 1941 everything in the world changed, especially in Hawaii. President Franklin D. Roosevelt's Declaration of War announced the beginning of a new agenda in business, industry, society and family life throughout America. Nothing was ever the same again. Americans had endured the Great Depression through the thirties and while many people struggled to earn a living, life seemed to be more innocent. There was a naivete that through the War years was dramatically lost.

The Wai'oli Tea Room was closed to the public during the war but the kitchen was used constantly to prepare meals and baked goods for military and civilian personnel throughout the Island of Oahu. Salvation Army USO (United Service Organizations) canteens distributed sandwiches and doughnuts and coffee nightly to sentry posts. All Salvation Army personnel on the island during the war were involved in serving the Armed Forces either in nightly rounds or at the airport canteen with the men leaving and arriving from foreign duty.

The war ended in 1945 but business in Hawaii did not turn-on as suddenly as it had turned-off. It was several years before the tourist industry picked up enough momentum for the Tea Room's reopening to be announced.

The Tea Room was completely renovated before its reopening in 1947. The wrought iron tables with glass tops, and the chairs were refinished by the same company that had made them in 1920-21. The original wall murals done by J. Babcock, were cleaned by staff of a Honolulu artist recommended by the Museum. Babcock was a museum caliber artist. No one would attempt to "touch up" after water stains; a result of closure during the war. The scenes were from the G.N. Wilcox home area on Kauai. The artist had been commissioned for this work by

17

Pictured are Captains Larder and McKeown, Honolulu 1943.

Mr. Wilcox, himself. It is not known exactly when these wall murals disappeared. They were intact at the time of the Tea Room reopening after World War II.

As administrator of The Salvation Army's Children's Home, Captain Don Pitt played a major role in the reopening of the Wai'oli Tea Room after the war in 1947. His successor, Captain Muriel Mitchell, spoke highly of his administration during a time when traditional programming at the Children's Homes' had begun to change. There was becoming a noticeable change in the family profile of many children being admitted for care and the role of the Tea Room in the day-to-day activities of the Children's Home was weakening. The Salvation Army saw Mitchell's prior experience on the Home staff as a real benefit to strengthening the relationship between the Tea Room operation and the Children's Home. She knew they were not separate entities. The Tea Room was built for the purpose of training children and young women living in the Home and had served that purpose well for twenty-five years, at that time. Captain Mitchell served as Administrator for the Children's Homes' until 1955.

ANN LEAK

*I*t was a beautiful day, as usual, in Waikiki and The Salvation
Army divisional commander, Brigadier Arthur Brewer, was
enjoying a relaxed lunch at a coffee shop on Kalakaua
Avenue. Dining alone, his interest was taken with one of the servers
(waitress) working his area. An attractive mature woman, she seemed to
fly from one table to another without fuss or confusion. This observa-
tion reminded him of a recent discussion regarding the eventual hiring
of a manager for the Wai'oli Tea Room. He watched her for considerable

time and as the noon rush hour was nearly
past, he engaged her in conversation. He
asked her, simply, if she would ever consider
managing the Wai'oli Tea Room up in
Manoa Valley. They exchanged the usual
pleasantries and asked questions back and
forth. She went on with her duties, but in a
short time returned with an answer, "I
would like that very much," she said. She
was hired immediately by The Salvation
Army and thus began her legendary career

Ann Leak

as the first non-Salvation Army officer manager of the Wai'oli Tea
Room. The year was 1944. World War II was still raging in Europe and
in the Pacific. The Tea Room was still closed to the public but was used
almost daily in the preparation of food for distribution to military service personnel on the Island of Oahu. Ann used this time to become
acquainted with the facility and with The Salvation Army, in general.
She supervised the renovation that was to follow and worked very closely
with Captain Don Pitt in the reopening.

The Children's Chapel 1957. Youngsters of The Salvation Army Children's Home hold regular services in this chapel. It is also used for weddings.

In Muriel Mitchell's opinion, Ann Leak was a most unusual woman. Her background in food services was impressive. She had come to Honolulu during the war following the sudden death of her husband in San Francisco. She knew how to run a busy dining room, and she learned to balance all of her responsibilities. In the years when Wai'oli was closed to the public, she became acquainted with Honolulu's business and social community, all of which put her in good stead for attention to the Tea Room that was to follow. Effecting a higher profile for the Tea Room was always at the forefront of Ann's planning. She knew that without sufficient business the training activities would flag and she was determined to keep that from happening.

Some years after the Tea Room reopened, Ann Leak implemented a plan that she was sure would bring more visitors to the site. The Children's Chapel was an important feature of interest to all who visited

Wai'oli. It was a beautiful stone structure but to Ann's way of thinking, it lacked "color." She had a plan!

Erika Karawina was a regular patron at the Tea Room, bringing guests or enjoying an Afternoon Tea by herself and Ann came to know her as a friend. Karawina was a noted artist specializing in stained glass windows. With a bit of Ann Leak persuasion an agreement was made to fill the window openings of the chapel with stained glass. Karawina waived her usual fee for such an order, charging only for the materials needed. When the project was finished the chapel seemed to glow with new life. Ann continued to develop her plan with brochures, post cards and letters and within the year tours included the chapel as a major part of the Wai'oli Tea Room visit. In 1957 one of her new brochures contained the following text:

THE STORY OF THE WAI'OLI CHAPEL WINDOWS

Wai'oli Chapel's six stained glass windows tell Biblical stories in the interracial language of Hawaii. Because Wai'oli Chapel was built for children in The Salvation Army Children's Home, designs which are significant to them were selected for the windows.

New aspects of color are seen in the windows with every changing phase of light. In the early morning, the East windows glow and sparkle; the West side lights up in the afternoon. During certain hours there is an intriguing play of reflected light.

The windows were designed and executed by Erika Karawina (Mrs. Stanley C. Hsiao), Honolulu artist. Hers is the story of three continents—Europe by birth, Asia by marriage and America by choice. Born in Germany, she received her art training in Europe and New England.

Her work is in the permanent collections of the Boston Museum of Fine Arts, Worchester Art Museum, the Addison Gallery of American Art at Andover, Massachusetts, the Metropolitan Museum of New York, the Museum of Modern Art, the Library of Congress, and Honolulu Academy of Arts, as well as in many private collections.

THE CHILDREN'S WINDOW: This window at the rear of the chapel was dedicated by Erika to all the children of the islands who have been her inspiration. It depicts the childhood of Jesus. Notice the Polynesian angels in *muumuu* and *pareau*, the Alii among the Magi and St. Joseph in a coconut hat.

ANN LEAK WINDOW: The window near the altar speaks of Christ's Passion. It was a gift by the employees of the Tea Room in honor of the manager Ann Leak, who worked devotedly for many years for The Salvation Army at Wai'oli.

NOAH'S ARK WINDOWS: The four side windows tell the story of the great flood. In the first section, the ark is floating on the water and it is raining. A half moon is the symbol of night, darkness

The Children's Window

and calamity. A blue band filled with romping animals, mongoose and water buffalo as well as kangaroos and elephants–carries the eye around to the opposite side wall. There the ark is finally resting on the mountaintop. Noah, with outstretched arms, beholds the dove with the olive branch, and the rainbow, symbol of God's covenant with man.

THE SIDE WINDOWS ARE DEDICATED TO:

• **George Norton Wilcox,** to whose generosity The Salvation Army is greatly indebted;

• **Commandant Rachel Payne,** Salvation Army officer, founder of the Wai'oli Tea Room; and

• **Visitors to this Chapel** whose gifts have made these windows possible.

Ann Leak left a legacy in her nurturing of children. She was a "firecracker," full of energy; a dynamic personality, Muriel Mitchell related. She was a real worker, on the job every morning by 5:30 and went non-stop all day, except to change her shoes. Brigadier Bram Collier had been appointed the new Divisional Commander and with his arrival came a new order in the day-to-day operation of Waiʻoli.

(left) The Ann Leak Window
(below) Noah's Ark Windows

Ann Leak is pictured with Miungo Lee Hall in front of the window dedicated to her by the employees.

Captain Muriel Mitchell, Home Administrator 1947–55 with Ann Leak, Wai'oli Manager 1947–62, Captain Sybil Barry of Divisional Headquarters 1955.

Divisional Headquarters took on the supervisory role of the Tea Room, relieving the Girls' Home administration of the responsibility. Ann Leak remained dedicated to the Army and especially the Girls' Home. Her attitude reflected her feelings that nothing was ever too much for her to do for the children.

Captain Muriel Mitchell shared Ann Leak's approach as to the original and continuing purpose of the Wai'oli Tea Room; that unless the effort was making a direct contribution to the children, the Tea Room was failing. The making of money was not her major priority. She felt that the Tea Room activity had to be helping the Home and the children. In the years prior to the war, older girls of the Home worked in the Tea Room after school serving Afternoon Tea. When the Tea Room reopened in the late forties, a luncheon service became standard fare requiring a more strict mode of operation and service. It seemed that since the war, older girls in the home were exhibiting a more complex set of behaviors and it soon became evident that they were opposed to working in the Tea Room at all, even for the fifty cents an hour that was offered. Ann's patience was tried to the limit, necessitating a change in work assignments for girls from the Home who had become indifferent

Students take notes during a pie-baking session. (Salvation Army photo) Girls in the classes wore aprons and head bands.

and resentful. Baking Classes were conducted for those who wanted to learn and it was primarily the younger aged girls who were keenly interested. Eventually the classes were opened to young women in the neighborhood. Little boys who lived on the home's Manoa campus were also a part of these classes if they had sisters in The Children's Home.

When live television began in Hawaii, a local station frequently invited the children's baking class to come to the studio kitchen and show their skills in cooking from "scratch."

One day a member of The Salvation Army's Advisory Board called the office of the Girls Home about his eight-year old daughter and a dinner-table conversation at their home the night before. He said they were sharing the news of the sudden death of the mother in a family of one of their relatives. After some moments of silence, he added, his daughter spoke up and said "If both of my parents died I could go to

The boys wore white jackets and chef hats. Mrs. Leak was always very close-by.

live at The Salvation Army Girls' Home and work in Wai'oli Tea Room every day. They do a lot of fun things there."

A gift to the teenage girls in 1952 was the "Dorothy Carnegie Course of Charm and Poise" conducted right in their cottage one night a week for eight weeks. A fashion show and dinner at the Tea Room was their graduation exercise. The fashions came from a lovely dress shop in Waikiki and the dinner was prepared by the girls in the baking class. Guests watched the show from tables placed throughout the dining rooms. Each of the girls was allowed to invite two guests to the dinner.

These special dinners were planned for three times a year with the baking class doing everything including the invitations. The girls were free to invite any guests they wished; usually teachers, social workers, families, staff members. The dinners were always successful affairs and drew the surprised interest of families of the Manoa Valley neighborhood children.

Ann was a perfectionist with her employees and business associates. But with the children, while she insisted on things being done properly,

Ann Leak with (then) Major Henry Koerner receiving the 25 Year Award from Roy H. Park of the Duncan Hines Institute, 1947. A large original watercolor painting depicting a full house on the dining lanai at Wai'oli Tea Room was presented.

there was a softer and more loving side of her nature clearly revealed and to which the children responded whole-heartedly. She had said very often, "The children are the reason I am working."

She became a committed devotee of The Salvation Army while a member of the Russian Orthodox Church. She was held in high esteem by her peers, and Ann gave so much in developing the Wai'oli Tea Room. She was always clear to point out with her public associations that Wai'oli Tea Room was a Salvation Army operation.

A special feature that accompanied the luncheon experience at Wai'oli during Ann Leak's years was the mingling of Hawaiian voices as a group of waitresses sang the Doxology in the Hawaiian language at noontime everyday. Small cards were put at each table outlining the words for any patrons who wished to join in.

Ann Leak retired in 1962 and moved to Sun City, Arizona where she died c. 1993. Captain Muriel Mitchell married Lt. Colonel Bram Collier and now retired, resides in Sun City West, Arizona.

A PRESENCE FROM THE PAST

*R*achel Payne had retired from active work with The Salvation Army in 1928 and, nineteen years later, she was still a very energetic personality, according to Captain Mitchell. Mitchell went on to say that she was a very private person, making it difficult to establish a real friendship. She added that it was five years into their acquaintance before she shared stories of the early days of Waiʻoli, and subsequent invitation to her "House of Stone" on the hill. Over a cup of tea she shared her recollections of personality struggles

with colleagues in her efforts to improve the children's home. She told of her close friendship with George Wilcox and of his frequent visits to Honolulu to survey the property with which he was so involved. She talked about the building of the Boys' Home in 1916, first on the Manoa

The House of Stone

campus and later in Kaimuki, and the growing need for specialized services with so many children who had never known any real family life and the love of parents.

This "house of stone" as she so lovingly referred to it, was built in 1928 specifically for Rachel Payne and her associate officer, Major Carrie Sabine. It was, purportedly, a retirement gift from G.N. Wilcox. The Salvation Army assured Wilcox that the two women would be given residence there for as long as they lived. It remains a Salvation Army property; a staff residence for administrative officers. It was a unique structure with all exterior walls made of stone (Moss rock). It was built as a modified duplex with two separate sections, a common living area and kitchen, and an open lanai overlooking the tropical gardens on the rise of Mt. Tantalus. It is almost hidden in the trees way up behind the Tea Room buildings. A remarkable screened door secured the residence. It was made of wrought iron and had a very strong locking system. Within the door's frame a decorative pattern depicted a spider and a fly from the old story... "Come into my parlor, said the spider to the fly..." It measured 3' by 7' to the top of the curved frame.

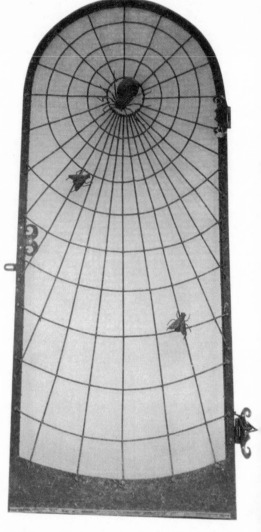

1928 wrought iron screen door with decorative pattern depicting the spider and a fly.

The screen door was removed in 1966 when the house was remodeled to a single family residence. The open lanai was screened and serves as a sitting porch and entry; the door was moved to the outside portico.

Rachel Payne died in 1955. She had lived a long productive life as a Salvation Army officer. She is buried in The Salvation Army Girls' Home plot in the Makiki Cemetery at Pensacola and Wilder Streets in Honolulu, not far from the Manoa Valley where she served at

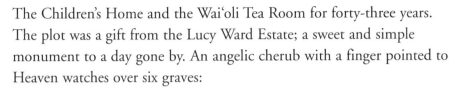

The Children's Home and the Waiʻoli Tea Room for forty-three years. The plot was a gift from the Lucy Ward Estate; a sweet and simple monument to a day gone by. An angelic cherub with a finger pointed to Heaven watches over six graves:

- **Baby Beth**
- **Baby Martha**
- **Mary Ah Choy**
  September 3, 1915–September 14, 1929
- **Isaac Ozaki**
  Son of Ensign and Mrs. Ozaki
  December 10, 1922–July 16, 1926

- **Major Carrie Sabine**
  December 1, 1868–February 28, 1939
- **Commandant Rachel Payne**
  December 6, 1875–July 25, 1955

At the head of the Tea Room's Memorial Garden a very large stone bears a bronze marker in remembrance of Rachel Payne's contribution to the children of Hawaii.

In the mid to late 1930's several dormitory buildings on the property were razed to make ready for new construction. By that time the Community Chest, a combined community fund-raising effort for non-profit programs, removed the Army's direct access to private citizens for financial contributions. As a member of the Community Chest, The Salvation Army agreed to abide by the rules, relying very much on the Community Chest Annual Drive for funds. Their allocation was never enough, and to meet the needs of the Home, a portion of The Girls' Home property on the opposite side of Oahu Avenue was sold to the City of Honolulu.

George N. Wilcox

With funds from the sale of the property, a gymnasium was built on the flat land adjacent to Cooke Cottage. Kamakana Cottage was renamed "Dillingham Cottage," the name it retained until it, too, was replaced by the new buildings in 1956. Cooke Cottage and Wilcox Cottage were also razed in the new building era of the mid-Fifties.

Some stone walls and foundations of old buildings are still in evidence around the Manoa property, subtle reminders of The Salvation Army's original purpose in the care of children; providing more than shelter, but a firm foundation for life with an awareness that God loves them.

YEARS IN TRANSITION

*T*he Waiʻoli Tea Room served its originally intended purpose for more than forty years; vocational training for maturing young women in residence at The Salvation Army Girls' Home. In the late Fifties The Salvation Army's work with children underwent a reorganization and distanced the Tea Room's viable training with young people in residence at the Children's Home. The reason given for the withdrawal of children from the Tea Room operation was related to the therapeutic treatment involved in serving children with emotional and behavioral disturbances. The Tea Room staff were trained in food services. By 1966 there were few, if any, children from the Home working at the Tea Room. Many workers at Waiʻoli were now long-term employees of The Salvation Army. Federal minimum wage laws and many employee benefit programs had not yet been enacted. Costs were relatively low and production was high. Business was good!

Following Ann Leak's retirement in 1962, Captain Hope Guernsey was appointed manager of the Tea Room. Coming from a Salvation Army appointment in Redondo Beach, California, she had an excellent reputation as a creative and gracious hostess with good management skills. She served well for four years, making every effort to maintain the reputation that the Leak years had established. Captain Guernsey served as manager from 1962 to 1966.

Guernsey's leaving in 1966 led to a lease agreement by The Salvation Army with Leo Qualls, dba Tantalus Enterprises, Inc. Approval was given for a lease to be drawn up with an established restaurateur known by then Divisional Commander Brigadier Frank Moss. The Tea Room had not been leased before this time.

Open salad bars were becoming popular alternatives to full-service dining, especially on luncheon menus, and it wasn't long before there was an elaborate salad bar selection being offered at Wai'oli Tea Room. It caught on and continued to be a major dining attraction on Wai'oli's menu for many years.

Qualls moved the Tea Room into evening dining with the addition of a dinner menu. To

Captain Hope Guernsey, Brigadier Eva Parkins, and Major Jean Cline pose with Ann Leak at her retirement in 1962.

improve the "after dark" ambience, gas lines were laid throughout the property within close proximity to the main building, and soon thereafter, tiki torches pierced the black night sky. These may have controlled some of the evening mosquito problem, as well. The evening dining experience was short lived; some speculating that The Salvation Army's policy on alcohol abstinence may have had a bearing on this venture. Mr. Qualls maintained the bakery at full scale and, as usual, hundreds of pounds of fruitcake was produced at Christmas time. The gift shop interior was improved and stock increased, providing a broader assortment of souvenirs for visitors to Wai'oli.

Many long-term staff continued to work through the years of the lease, striving to maintain the well-known Wai'oli tradition. The spirit and personality of Wai'oli was always an important part of its presentation. The menu carried only three entrees; Oven-fried Wai'oli Chicken, Deep-fried Coconut Mahi, and Stevenson Broil, a specially seasoned portion of lean ground beef, grilled to selected doneness. Each cut of fried chicken was exactly the same size, (a small half fryer) that always tasted the same; "*Ono!*" which in Hawaiian means "good." The Coconut Mahi and the Stevenson Broil maintained their popularity running close seconds to the chicken in popularity. The Robert Louis Stevenson Grass Shack helped in the naming of the beef offering.

8

MIUNGO LEE HALL

The Tantalus Enterprises lease was terminated in 1971, moving the Tea Room into another restart. It was well known that a respected Waiʻoli staff had remained intact throughout the course of the lease years. The naming of a new manager was once again the plight of The Salvation Army. Who better to bring it back to its original presentation than a faithful member of its old staff; Lee Hall. Miungo Lee Hall was 18 years old when she came to The Girls' Home from Hilo during the War. She worked in an office of military business, then temporarily located at Punahou School not far from Waiʻoli Tea Room. When the Tea Room reopened in 1947, Lee held major positions progressing through the ranks from managing the kitchen, to the gift shop and the dining rooms. She knew it all and she, too, wanted to have Waiʻoli's image maintained, if not restored, to what Mrs. Leak had worked so hard to develop. Almost ten years had passed since Leak's retirement and Miungo had seen the business change over the years. The hillside's constant ground movement was a maintenance nightmare. Repairs to the fifty-year-old buildings had been made haphazardly. The gardens needed daily attention. The trees were dangerously overgrown and the walkways were covered with a mossy growth for lack of sunlight.

The Salvation Army saw Miungo Lee Hall as the perfect candidate for manager; a veteran employee who could bring the Tea Room back to its once famous stature in the local and the world community. She accepted the position in 1972. Lee was a "hands on" manager, working long hours to fulfill what she saw as her responsibilities.

Visitors were becoming much more demanding and the sporadic tour bus traffic only complicated the frustrations of "gracious dining." Waiʻoli was located too near to town to be a regular luncheon stop for

Miungo Lee Hall 1976.

the buses, but drop-by bus tours unloaded hundreds of people at a time onto the otherwise serene landscape. Whereas many businesses were compensating the bus drivers for stopping, Wai'oli could not. Buses stopped anyway, as friendly drivers enjoyed complimentary coffee and pastry with the Wai'oli workers. In addition, a welcome feature was a restroom stop for their passengers headed over the Pali to a luncheon destination further away. Wai'oli's uniqueness with the wedding chapel and the grass hut made it an attraction for the tour companies who could include it as a short stop even on a half-day tour. Few bus visitors knew anything of Wai'oli's history, and it's anybody's guess what the drivers may have told them. Pouring off the big ten-wheel motor coaches they scurried through the gardens with cameras dangling off both shoulders, snapping pictures of everything in view. Despite markers and verbal admonitions, visitors plucked blossoms and wore them with a flair over one or the other of their ears. As many as eight coaches at one time filled the crowded parking lot on any given day during the height of the season and motors were left running to keep the air conditioning on, causing ugly exhaust fumes.

WAI'OLI TEA ROOM PRICES INCREASE
February 26, 1973

Fried Chicken Lunch increased to $3.00
Salad Luncheon increased to $2.60
Child Lunch to $2.25
Carrot Bread 2# loaf $1.75
Fruit Pies $2.00

A WOMEN'S AUXILIARY, chartered in 1969, was a strong support group of all Salvation Army activities on the Island of Oahu, and the Wai'oli Tea Room was always a special assignment for their volunteer services. Commencing in 1973 visitors were greeted by Auxiliary volunteers and served a complimentary cup of fruit punch as they moved through the entrance lanai. A "*calabash bowl*" was placed appropriately for free-will offerings in support of The Salvation Army. A crystal punchbowl was filled and refilled with a special blend of tropical fruit juices. Cups were arranged on a large ornate tile-topped teakwood table, a gift to Wai'oli by the Fleishmann Yeast family. The genteel practice of serving punch continued for many years marking Wai'oli indelibly as a distinctive spot filled with the spirit of *Aloha*. The punch service was discontinued when Department of Health regulations required that such an offering be served from a closed container, a commercial decanter. Along with the fact that donations had waned, something was lost in the translation from the open punchbowl to the urn and the service was discontinued.

LIBBY'S *LUA*

*T*his history would not be complete without at least a reference to "Libby's *Lua*" which effected a great improvement in Wai'oli's ambience around 1972. Replacing former restroom facilities in the Tea Room main building, a new lava rock structure was designed by architect Roland Libby Jr., to be built across the parking lot near the chapel. Libby donated his services based on his grandmother's love and services to The Salvation Army in Buffalo, N.Y. many years earlier. His own mother, Jane, a pioneer member of the Honolulu Women's Auxiliary, is a long-standing member of the Honolulu Advisory Board and served for many years on the Council of The Salvation Army's Children's Home (Residential Treatment Facilities) which closed in 1991.

MIUNGO LEE HALL SEEKS RETIREMENT

Showers and birthday parties filled the Saturday reservations. The bakery worked fulltime and business flourished on a roller-coaster basis. Lee was beginning to feel the pressures of the day-to-day work and asked The Salvation Army for a relief. It was 1978 and she wanted to retire. Major Glenn Austin, then Divisional Commander, understood Mrs. Hall's desire to let it go and could see the strain she was under. He knew the difficulty with management changes and Wai'oli Tea Room had experienced many, but he was eager to see the Tea Room operation continue without interruption.

During the summer of 1978 two former residents of Honolulu, Bob and Bette Stillwell, returned to Hawaii to make Kailua their home. Both were well known to The Salvation Army and much of the Honolulu community and while Dr. Bob went directly into a new position, Bette was looking forward to an at-home summer. Knowing her background in public relations and program management, The Salvation Army sought her involvement as interim manager for the Tea Room until more permanent leadership could be found. In September, Miungo Hall was duly honored at a civic retirement reception which was well attended by former Wai'oli staffers and friends. At its conclusion she presented Bette Stillwell with a heavy ring of keys to demonstrate the transfer of management responsibility and Bette was introduced as the new manager.

BETTE'S STORY

WAIOLI TEA ROOM

1978 ~ 1999

(clockwise from top left) 1982 Manager Bette Stillwell with staff; Brian Hood, Doug Stillwell, Phyllis Kolo, Teleise Ochoa, and Suk Cha Choe.

9

BETTE STILLWELL

*T*he Manager's parking place was waiting for me and my first day on the job was very exciting. I could hardly believe it! I had been charmed by this old place from first sight of it more than ten years earlier. My family remind me that I charged in to my new responsibilities like a warrior going into battle; I was hell-bent on maintaining the reputation Mrs. Hall had established and this effort called upon all of my resources from day one. Coming in new only magnified the building's need for major repairs. Dealing with the housekeeping and learning the overall business kept me in perpetual motion. The six years as "interim" manager became the most memorable and treasured work years of my life. Deferred maintenance, as I referred to it, was a constant drain on property reserves. The moisture of Manoa Valley had taken its toll on interior wall surfaces, some areas swollen and split apart in prominent locations in the dining rooms. Money

Bette Stillwell

seemed always to be directed to higher priority needs such as the payroll, utilities, and an unyielding inventory of food stores, supplies and equipment.

Wai'oli had a remarkable staff of workers who rallied daily, many before dawn. They were a humble crew, most working at minimum wage, but very dedicated. By 1978 many were long-term employees, having stayed on through many management styles. Twenty-year employee, Elsie Monma, was assistant manager. She ran the gift shop, handling purchasing, pricing, reservations, sales, accounting and more. Phyllis Kolo, a ten-year veteran, was in charge of the dining room, while she doubled in baking, cooking, gift shop when needed, and wherever else she was called. She prepared and served the Afternoon Teas. Elizabeth Haili, Alice Aylett, Rose Kaolelopono, Alma Lee, and Suk Cha Choe (Sukie) were mainstays, as well, seldom absent, always ready for work at a very early hour.

My son, Doug Stillwell, played a major role in my day-to-day pacing. He headed the maintenance work of the buildings and acres of grounds, under the supervision of Divisional Headquarters. His constant good nature, his permanent smile, and a happy whistle kept everyone in touch with his whereabouts. His

1983: Elsie Monma (left), Elizabeth Haili (right).

drop-in visits to my office with a little bunch of ginger blossoms could make my day. Doug was a master fixer, builder, mender, and landscape gardener. He worked hard and he worked fast. When the dining room "crush" was heavy, Doug changed his shirt, donned an apron, and washed his hands to buss tables, or dip ice cream cones, whistling all the while.

Doug Stillwell thatches the restored hut, now at The Salvation Army Tea Room.

There were many stars in this great cast and each one played a significant role in Waiʻoliʻs continuing saga. Chef-Baker David Weaver, another Chef-Baker Alden Kaleohano, Audrey Uyehara, Jennifer Hartman, Glenn Austin Jr., Joell and Brian Hood, Mark Morelock, Sammy Vera Cruz, Danny Souza and David Nehoa, to name a few. Gil Stewart, an energetic "haole boy" from California added much to the excitement of Waiʻoliʻs family in 1980. Through the summer many students joined the staff; Lani and Danny Abella, Debbie Domingo, Lori Gorlangton, Lionel Kaueakalau, Laurel Bronner, Eddie Daoang, Shawn Kaueakalau, Adam Morales, Patricia Ting, Nathan Haili, Chef – John Eddy, Lisa Kobayashi, Brengle Navarro, Gerald Ishihara, Jeanne Sullivan, Chef – Steve Papell, Julia McCormick, Roxana Chu, Lynn Ly, Warren Chun, Yvonne Yu, Hostess – Diane Hatori, Dean Kaneko, Keith Mills and Bonnie Takara. Waiʻoliʻs "*ohana*" was a great mix of people and personalities. Staff parties were always a wonderful time.

Hardly a day of business was lost during the renovations which began in 1980, a precursor to the major rebuilding of 1993. The roof was patched and sections of walls were replaced. The back terrace "patio roofing" which, in places, was too low for tall visitors, was replaced with a beamed ceiling.

As the old place was responding to its face-lifting, it seemed a good time for a promotional event surrounding Waiʻoliʻs Sixtieth Anniversary.

So, in September of 1981 we presented "The Waiʻoli Renaissance," an Afternoon Tea resplendent with all of Waiʻoli's famous sweets and savouries, lace cloths, the best silver, and masses of flowers everywhere. Hawaii's "treasure of song," Irmgard Aluli and Puamana (her own family) entertained. The hula was danced, and under the direction of Anuhea Brown, the Prince Kuhio Chorus performed.

Advisory Board Chairman Ted Damron introduced special guests which included Majors Kenneth and Barbara Hood, he the Divisional Commander, and Richard and Julia McAbee, accompanied by grandson Richard and fiancée Michelle, who had come from Seattle to attend and participate in the rededication program.

Richard McAbee was my mother's brother. His presence at this program was in direct response to his interest in the property and The Salvation Army Children's Home where from 1909 to 1912, his wife Julia, lived as a young child. Mr. McAbee was a significant contributor to my early sensitivity in recording this history. He provided much of the written historical detail and old photographs. I asked him to give the Dedicatory Prayer during the formal service. He died in Seattle April 3, 1999.

(Above) Artist Susan McGovney Hansen with Major Kenneth Hood.

Waioli Renaissance

1921-1981

The Salvation Army Waioli Tea Room · Honolulu, Hawaii

Dr. Robert Stillwell introducing program.   *Puamana wait to perform.*

DEDICATORY PRAYER – Wai'oli Tea Room
by F. Richard McAbee

"Dear Jesus…As we rededicate this land and these
facilities to Thy service, we ask for Thy continued
blessing and guidance for all that is done here. Grant
to those who are responsible for the renewal of these
structures the wisdom, guidance and understanding
that You gave to those in the beginning for a
children's home.

We thank Thee for the recognition the State officials
have shown for the care and shelter that made this
place a living monument in the memories of the
children and young people who lived on these
hallowed grounds during the past eighty-four years.
We are exceedingly grateful for those who have made
the remodeling and refurbishment possible and for
those who will contribute to its completion.

Be with those who devote themselves to its future, that
it shall always be an inspiration to those who visit and
enjoy the hospitality and warmth of affection shown
by those who serve here. May Thy Spirit continue to
touch the lives of all who participate in the renewal.
Our hearts and minds are filled with gratitude for
Your abiding love and ever-present help in our daily
lives. Amen."

It was a grand celebration, making it seem like everyone in Hawaii should know that the Waiʻoli Tea Room was alive and well.

An "Attic Sale" helped to clean out closets and storerooms. With a small newspaper ad announcing the sale, droves of people gathered early to stake their choices long before the stated hour. A poster contest was launched, sponsored by Holly Worrall, owner of the Manoa Gallery, with a prestigious panel of professional judges including artist John Young and architect/artist Vladimir Ossipoff. The winning entry was done by watercolorist Susan McGovney Hansen, entitled "Waiʻoli Renaissance," which best expressed Waiʻoli's "Aloha" for a supportive community. The poster has become a treasure to poster collectors the world over.

THE WAIʻOLI GARDENS

It wouldn't take many weeks of neglect for the gardens surrounding Waiʻoli to become a veritable jungle totally hiding the buildings. The ten acres requires daily attention to keep the plants and trees trimmed for maximum flowering and growth. The magnificent Congia (Sandpaper Vine) at the Tea Room's main entrance is in full bloom in the winter months. This unusual vine, said to have been transported from Malaya, has been the centerpiece of the entrance for thirty-five years; a mass of pale lavender forming a dramatic backdrop for color pictures. A Manoa friend and patron, Jane Fujimoto, had planted a slip when Ann Leak was the manager c. 1960. Many of the unusual plants throughout the grounds were gifts of Jane and she tended the gardens regularly, a dedicated volunteer who loved Waiʻoli and all that it stood for. Jane Fujimoto died in 1992.

A steel support was anchored to the old entry roofline in 1981, to hold the heavy growth that shaded the full side of the entrance. Clarence Ing, another treasured Salvation Army volunteer, lent his handiwork to building the new trellis. With the rebuilding of the entrance in 1993, the Congia was carefully transplanted a few feet further into the garden

(above) The maile is separated by Bette Stillwell, Waiʻoli Manager, with Major Barbara Hood and former manager, Miungo Lee Hall.

and continues to blossom in the bright Hawaiian sunlight from January through May.

The gardens were cataloged in 1981 awaiting the day when markers would be set for visitors to read and enjoy. Pruning of the trees was often delayed because of the high cost involved. The old Mango tree fronting the lanai was enormous. It was a constant challenge for the gardeners to keep plantings in its shade. There had been a time when dining on the lanai one could almost reach out and pluck a Mountain Apple, but with growth over many years now the apples are higher than the roof top.

The Macadamia Nut tree in the back garden had a brace positioned to give it support after its fall in 1982 hurricane winds. Enormous Monkeypod trees umbrella the entire property. The Coffee bushes are crowded by the banana plants sometimes obscuring a view of the Grass House from the terrace dining area. The old Cactus in the front garden, another gift of Jane Fujimoto, and the Autograph tree are strong and healthy. The Waiʻoli gardens were recognized in 1981 with a landscaping award given by The Outdoor Circle of Honolulu.

Some remnants of earlier days still remain; a little foot bridge spans a channel between the kitchen and the coffee hut with "Ann Leak" scribbled in the concrete. A bronze fish in the koi pond surround, and "Miungo" set in the cracked concrete flooring behind the kitchen. All are reminders of a day gone by.

WAI'OLI TEA ROOM GARDENS

Ala'ni
Aloe
Amaranthus (Pigweed)
Amaryllis
Ama'uma'u
Angel's trumpet
Anthurium
Areca palm
Autograph tree
Banana
Bird of paradise
Bixa (Lipstick)
Bleeding heart
Blue ginger
Bougainvillea
Bromeliad
Cactus
Camellia
Canna
Christmas berry
Coconut palms
Coffee
Congia
Erythrina
Fiddlewood
Guava

Hala, Pu hala, Screw pine
Hapu'u (Tree fern)
Hau
Hibiscus
Huapala
Ie'ie
Iliahialo'e
Ixora
Kiawe (Mesquite)
Koa haole
Koali (Morning glory)
Kopiko
Lantana
Lasiandra (Glory bush)
Liliko'i (Passion flower)
Limu
Macadamia nut
Mango
Manono
Marantaceae
Mexoneuron kuaiense
Moa
Mondo
Monkeypod
Monstera
Mountain apple
Naupaka
Norfolk pine

Oha
Ohelo
'Ohi'a lehua
Olopua
Orchid
Panaunau
Panax
Philodendron
Plumeria
Pukiawe
Red ginger
Sea grape
Seaside heliotrope
Shell ginger
Silk oak
Spider lily
Surinam cherry
Syngonium
Taro
Ti
Tree heliotrope
Uluhe
Waiawi 'ula'ula
Wood rose
Yellow allamanda

Before the end of 1983 a Sunday brunch service was introduced. Church bulletins became a coupon for brunch discounts and Sunday was a very happy day at Wai'oli. Let me say here that Salvation Army approval for the Sunday opening was a real surprise knowing the organization's reverence of the Sabbath Day. Salvation Army officers and church members became regular customers.

Christmas time was a "full house" season for luncheons, parties and bakery orders. Right after Thanksgiving the bakery began taking Christmas orders for fruitcakes, Christmas breads and cookies. Wai'oli Fruitcakes were a sell-out. The process started in November. Tubs of fruitcake batter were prepared every day, poured onto deep sheet pans and baked slowly. After cooling at least over night, they were cut into 8 oz, 1 pound and 2 pound pieces and wrapped in cellophane, tied with a red ribbon and carried the gold seal of Wai'oli Tea Room. This was the same fruitcake recipe used during the War years when thousands of pounds were prepared each Christmas, individually wrapped and distributed throughout Hawaii's military installations. In addition to the Military, a special contingent of Salvation Army personnel delivered fruitcakes to the Kalaupapa Center on the Island of Molokai. Members of the Women's Auxiliary spent many hours applying fancy Christmas wrap to the hundreds of pounds distributed to shut-ins, veterans hospitals and rest homes throughout the Island of Oahu. Times have changed. No longer is fruitcake considered a wise gift, especially for the elderly community. The cakes have been replaced with toiletry items.

Robert Louis Stevenson Memorial Grass House

"HISTORY ALTERED" accused by Honolulu Advertiser *Columnist Bob Krauss, in the demise and rebuilding of the Robert Louis Stevenson Grass Shack on Wai'oli grounds since the Twenties…*

 fter numerous insurance claims from falls on uneven ground, tripping off eroded walkways or bumping into a sagging tin roof

*1926 Robert
Louis Stevenson
Grass Shack*

on the old grass hut lanai, I had to recommend to Waiʻoli's Advisory
Council that the old grass hut (56 years in Waiʻoli's garden at that time)
be demolished and, if possible, rebuilt to provide a safer visitor environment. The demolition was approved wholeheartedly by Salvation Army
administration, but when the item hit the newspapers it was a different
story. Many local people remembered the placement of the hut from
Ainahau to Waiʻoli in the late twenties and others who didn't remember
were dismayed that this piece of history would be gone forever. I
received calls all day trying to explain the plight with the insurance
claims and the dangerous walkway surfaces around the hut. The fury
subsided eventually, and over the next six or seven months, an
unbelievable story unfolded.

Some years earlier the *Honolulu Advertiser* had carried an extensive
feature on the background and proper building of grass houses. I must
have had a premonition that I might need the information so I clipped
the article and put it in a file marked "RLS Grass House." The story
described the work of a noted architect who specialized in building grass
houses. With a little investigating I located and called Mr. Raymond
Morris, the noted architect. He seemed quite taken with my need and
set to work on plans. Meanwhile I received a call from a woman who
wished to remain anonymous but who was a "fan" of anything

1983: (l to r) Major Mervyn Morelock, Architect Ray Morris demonstrates pili grass tying, Mel Darneal, Doug Stillwell, and Bette Stillwell.

Princess Ka'iulani and Robert Louis Stevenson. She asked how much money we would need to rebuild the hut as soon as possible. When the plans were completed, materials listed, and a skilled builder found, I began to tally the costs for 1000 feet of straight *ohia* logs, a truck load of *pili* grass, some sawed lumber despite the architect's objections, paving stones for a lanai, and related hardware that was needed.

Morris remembered seeing the dismantled house in 1926… There were no sawed timbers as there were in the house just prior to its most recent restoration. By searching the state archives, it was determined that the house began as a simple thatched structure. A primitive lanai was added, then windows and later a more elegant lanai. The porch was changed again when the house was moved to Wai'oli, due, probably, to the sloping of the ground. The restorers decided to go back to a 1890s photograph showing friends of Kaiulani lounging in front of the structure *(see page 7)*.

The donor invited Mr. and Mrs. Morris to accompany me to her home which sat on a sheer cliff above the ocean in Honolulu's exclusive Black Point area. We sipped lemonade and talked about the grass house. Getting right to the point, she agreed to finance the entire project with payments being made throughout completion phases. Morris secured a building permit; we had to do this right! Mel Darneal who had worked with Morris on other building projects was hired as the head carpenter and preliminary site preparation was under the direction of carpenter assistant, Doug Stillwell. Many of Wai'oli's regular employees volunteered their time before and after work schedules to assist with the project. First the old hut had to be torn apart and disposed of and truckloads of debris were hauled away every day until the plot was cleared and ready for work to begin.

Hawaii's Waioli Tea Room

Link with Robert Louis Stevenson

Where The Salvation Army Serves the People of Many Lands

By Senior-Captain DON PITT

Article that ran in the 1951 issue of "All The World."

The 1,000 feet of Ohia logs were harvested by inmates of the Kulani Prison Farm of the Big Island and shipped to Oahu by barge. Thatching of *pili* grass from Molokai and plaiting or weaving of coconut fronds and hala leaves are almost lost crafts but I was able to find two men who could do the work. Another window was cut in the building to make the interior more viewable.

Formal groundbreaking ceremonies were held in February of 1983 for the new Robert Louis Stevenson Memorial Grass House. The ground had been prepared for building to commence and the invitation to attend was circulated to members of The Salvation Army Advisory Board and Advisory Councils. Board Chairman, Ted Damron, opened the festive event with introduction of notables in attendance: Colonel and Mrs. Will Pratt of Territorial Headquarters in Los Angeles, Majors

Mervyn and Shirley Morelock, he
the Divisional Commander at
that time, Phyllis Fox, then
Executive Director of the Historic
Hawaii Foundation, Mr. Bob
Krauss with the *Honolulu
Advertiser* and close monitor of
any and all things "historic" on
the property, and the Reverend
Abraham Akaka who would offer
a dramatic blessing on the new
project. Ray and Aldyth Morris
were present for the ritual, and
Mel Darneal and Doug Stillwell
were part of the program. At the
bidding of Morris, the ground-

Rev. Abraham Akaka–Bette holds koa bowl.

breaking ceremony concluded with the singing of a traditional hymn,
"Hawaii Aloha." It had been a wonderful day that set the tone for a full
year of excitement. For the next three months the project attracted
scores of people to the property every day to watch things develop.

The benefactor showed up unexpectedly from time to time, to
check things out for herself, as well. With a few variations necessary, like
fire protection sprinklers on the roof and electricity for maintenance and
lighting as needed, the building proceeded on schedule and the days
passed quickly.

A royal dedication program was set for May, 1983, with a
ho'o lau le'a (a grand Hawaiian party and feast) attended by Salvation
Army Territorial officials, Divisional officers, City of Honolulu officials
and State of Hawaii Representatives. History would be maintained,
albeit in a memorial sense.

From Off Duty/America/ January 1984

Little Grass Shack: A Piece of History is recreated in Manoa Valley

By Richard Cornwell

Originally, the famous Robert Louis Stevenson Grass Hut is said to have served as a playhouse for Princess Ka'iulani and her childhood friends, or a party house for Hawaiian royalty, a retreat for Robert Louis Stevenson, a honeymoon cottage, a nursery and, for the last 50 years, a major tourist attraction. In 1982 it was torn down. The "little grass shack" had deteriorated to where it was unsafe and its owners, the Salvation Army, didn't have funds to restore it.

How did the Salvation Army come to own this last of the grass houses? The little hut was built by Archibald Cleghorn, husband to a Hawaiian princess and father of Princess Ka'iulani, the favorite niece of Queen Liliuokalani. It was located adjacent to the main villa at Ainahau, the family's fairy-tale estate in what is now Waikiki's International Marketplace.

In the late Twenties when Ainahau was being sold, the historic grass shack was dismantled and offered to the highest bidder. The Salvation Army had opened the Wai'oli Tea Room in Manoa Valley as an adjunct to their girls (orphanage) home and the commander Rachel Payne had the foresight to realize that visitors might like to see the building. She won out over a farmer who wanted the hut for a chicken coop and she "transplanted" it to the lush Wai'oli grounds. There is no charge to visit the house and throngs of tourists still stop by to see it, have lunch or tea, stroll the grounds and shop for homemade jams, jellies, candies and tea breads in the gift shop.

Faced with restoring the grass house, manager Bette Stillwell contacted Honolulu columnist Bob Krauss, who made it a pet project. Shortly after the publicity

"ODE TO A LITTLE GRASS HOUSE"
Written by Bette M. Stillwell, Waiʻoli Tea Room 1983

A princess, a poet, a legend of fame...
Robert Louis Stevenson gave it a name.

From Ainahau–a pile of sticks
    rebuilt the house in '26,

Set on a knoll where all could see
    in Waiʻoli's garden while having tea.

Some doubt the stories of revelry
    linked to the writer of poetry;

Through many years of wind and rain,
    tropic sun–a hurricane...

With sagging eaves and thatch disheveled,
    time and termites finally leveled.

Manoa's landmark disappeared...
    Disappointment, yea, some tears...

"Save the house–It's got to stay!
    Call the press–We'll find a way!"

The word went out...a friend replied...
    "Build another and keep the pride."

Ohia logs–1000 feet. *Pili* grass in bundles neat.

Sand and rock foundation strong.
    Some insist we did it wrong...

But build it we did with struts and rails,
    ridge and plates and common nails.

And once again the house evolved...
    all the details now resolved.

Let the cameras and fans ascend
    and may her legends never end!

(top) Oil painting of Grass House. (above) Irmgard and Puamana.

Krauss gave the sad state of affairs, an anonymous donor phoned Mrs. Stillwell and asked how much it would cost to restore the house. (It seemed Princess Kaʻiulani had been a childhood idol of the prospective benefactor.) Retired architect Ray Morris, a Hawaiian resident for 64 years, offered to do the architectural work without charge to the Salvation Army. To begin with, he said he did not build shacks…he built houses…even grass houses.

WAIʻOLI: A UNIQUE WORK PLACE

*I*n the years just prior to my arrival as manager, the Waiʻoli Tea Room had become a work site for workers placed through the State Department of Labor; men and women who were minimally skilled but who worked hard and responded to respect. One such employee will always be remembered with much aloha…His name was "Sammy." He loved Mrs. Stillwell, "da boss lady!" One Saturday morning when Sammy's other chores were finished he asked me if there was something else I needed him to do like, perhaps, washing my car? I thought that was a splendid idea and I instructed him to "go ahead,"… and as he turned and walked away, I added…"start with the inside!"

Saturdays were often the busiest day of the week and by the end of the day I was ready to head to Kailua for two days at home. In my customary hurried manner, after opening the driver door of my little Datsun wagon, I flung my hand bag across the front seat and got in behind the wheel. Settling in I quickly came to attention realizing that my back and seat were becoming soaking wet. My long *muumuu* tucked around my knees was off the car's floor. Gingerly I let myself out of the vehicle to survey the situation and discovered the whole interior of the car was saturated. I remembered suddenly that Sammy loved to use a hose. I had instructed him to "wash the car…and start with the inside," and follow the orders he did! All I could do was shake my head in amusement. The thirty minute ride over the Pali was wetter than usual, and trying to keep my sense of humor, I chalked the experience up to "on-the-job training." After changing into some dry clothes I found a plug in the bottom of the spare tire well and drained that portion, but it was weeks before the car was dry again, even with daily removal of all the seats and mats to outside exposure.

Another remarkable story…Suk Cha had come to Hawaii the teen-aged Korean bride of a young man of American-Samoan ancestry. She spoke no English but determined to make a new life for herself away from her home country. The marriage did not last and from time to time she became part of the Stillwell family. Suki started work at the Wai'oli Tea Room in 1977, one of two full-time restaurant jobs that kept her busy from dawn 'til midnight. She learned quickly and was a tireless worker, running, never walking. Suki's sweet warmth with the patrons endeared her to dozens who always asked to be seated in her section. She was a ray of sunshine on a cloudy day. She learned to speak English from her peers with "pidgin" English taking the lead.

Assistant manager, Elsie Monma, supervised all of the employees and carried the respect of every worker. Her consistent manner and ability to stay "cool" under stress set an excellent example for her peers. She informed Suki that "pidgin" was never used when dealing with the public or speaking with Salvation Army staff members. Suki took her cue from senior staffer, Phyllis Kolo. With two full-time jobs, Suki maintained an uncanny charm with the world. She applied for and received US citizenship within two years. She did business with a local bank, saving almost every penny she made. Through frugal discipline she was able to bring her parents from Korea to live with her in a small condominium apartment she purchased in the Kapahulu district near Waikiki. Now more than twenty years later, Suki is her same perky self and can be seen any day at one of her Waikiki jobs.

"REMEMBERING 1983"

he following dissertation; a log of activity through the year, was presented at the employee Christmas party. It accompanied my annual report to the Salvation Army.

January roared in with a big wind that downed the Macadamia Nut Tree in the Stevenson garden. "Not to worry…!" Doug cried. He cut off broken branches easing the weight and reset the base with the strong support. Within a few weeks new growth could be seen. Plans were in place for the new grass house ground-breaking and many off-hours were filled by Waiʻoliʻs younger workers, helping to prepare the wooded area for the big event.

Groundbreaking ceremonies took the February spotlight, with Reverend Abraham Akaka officiating. He was assisted by Commissioner Will Pratt, Colonel Kenneth Hood, Major Mervyn Morelock – Divisional Commander, and Advisory Board Chairman Ted Damron. Distinguished guests present included Ray and Aldyth Morris, project architect, and Bob Krauss of the *Honolulu Advertiser*. The Historic Hawaii Foundation was represented by Phyllis Fox, Executive Director. The ceremonies were followed with a gala Tea Party.

March saw the commencement of construction as carpenter Mel Darneal and his apprentice, Doug Stillwell, set to work to reproduce an authentic grass house which, hopefully, would stand for years to come where the little original had stood since 1926.

In May a *"hoʻolauʻlea"* celebrated the completion of the project with a formal dedication of the Robert Louis Stevenson Memorial Grass House. This very special function was tied-in with the annual meeting of the Salvation Army Advisory Board of Honolulu.

Wai'oli garden lawn becomes stage for Kahiko *(ancient) hula.*

A brass band of the Salvation Army's Kauluwela
Mission Corps in Honolulu, the Royal Court of the
Aloha Week Festival, *Kahiko* (hula) dancers and
"*muumuu'd*" timbrelists brought color and excitement
to an otherwise serene hillside. A *luau* followed in the
Hawaiian tradition.

A debt of gratitude is owed to the anonymous donor
who provided all of the funds for the Grass House
Project, desiring to maintain a spirit of Robert Louis
Stevenson and the Royal Princess Ka'iulani for generations yet to come.

All will remember "Dark Wednesday," July 13th,
when a power outage shut down electricity all across
the Island of Oahu, allegedly started by a rampant
cane fire in the Waianae area.

Thanksgiving-time turned Wai'oli's kitchen into a fast-
paced "pie house" for twenty-four hours as Phyllis
Kolo and her crew put together 400 Pumpkin Pies for
the 2,000 portions that would be served at The
Salvation Army's Community Thanksgiving Dinner
held the next day at Neil Blaisdell Center in Honolulu.

Now it's Christmas Time... and my brain kicks into prose...

"The sun is shining – The sky is blue –
The gardens like emeralds with morning dew –
A million leaves with a different light...
Moving shadows of birds in flight..."

Wai'oli is alive with happy sounds, the kitchen strewn with cake and pie tins in preparation of orders for 200 individually wrapped cakes for delivery to Kalaupapa, Molokai and individual orders for fruitcakes, Christmas Stollen, quick breads and pies for the holidays.

The second annual Manager's Tea honored the people who helped to accomplish **WAI'OLI** – 1983; outstanding citizens, board and auxiliary members, staff members, employees and some very special customers. An "Academy of Awards" was staged and recipients bowed for "best performance" in their respective fields.

From my previous work with volunteers and line staff I had learned the importance and value of recognition of work well done. This initiated an event that would accomplish the goal with meaning and humor. It was nearing Christmas. Everyone was in the Holiday spirit and this was a perfect time for a comical, but sincere, "Thank You!"

With the colors and excitement of Christmas as the backdrop, guests were received in the Kauai Dining Room at the traditional Afternoon Tea Time to enjoy an array of sweets and savories with hot tea or cranberry punch. Antique embroidered tablecloths (a gift from Brigadier Nola Champion, Salvation Army Booth Home 1957) draped the long buffet table. Adding to the table's rich appearance was Wai'oli's silver tea service, a gift from the Salvation Army Women's Auxiliary of Honolulu in 1981, plus trays, pitchers and silver punch bowl, also a part of the auxiliary gift. A centerpiece of Pine, Eucalyptus, *Protea* and Christmas berries brought a scent of Christmas, and was carried through with evergreen boughs and candles on individual tables.

Guests were greeted and their roles in Wai'oli's history were defined as each related to Wai'oli's past, present, or future. I opened the party with the following:

> "Wai'oli is much more than a place…Wai'oli is people…All kinds of people working together in a unique aura of friendship from day to day…keeping a spirit of aloha alive and apparent to all who pass her way!"

Representing Christmases past were Beatrice Krauss and Gwenfread Allen two of Hawaii's most outstanding women. Through their professional careers, each of them made an indelible mark in Hawaii's cultural history. Krauss had been present at the 1922 dedication of The Wai'oli Tea Room; she was a neighbor in Manoa Valley, a retired ethnobotanist for HSPA (Hawaiian Sugar Planters Association), plant pathologist, Lyon Arboretum consultant, University of Hawaii professor and local historian. Her presence was, indeed, representative of the past. Krauss died in March of 1998 in her mid-nineties.

Gwenfread Allen was one of Honolulu's most distinguished writers, historians, and philanthropists, and had been a public relations staff writer for The Salvation Army in the Fifties. Her presence was equally representative of the past.

Representing Christmas Present…

Rose Marie Holmes provided classical piano melodies surrounding the season. Awards were presented as envelopes containing names of recipients and category descriptions were read by Wai'oli's most enthusiastic volunteer, Dr. Robert Stillwell.

For Best Performance as a Director in a limited series, documentary: Mr. **Ray Morris**, Architect, RLS Memorial Grass House Project

For Best Performance as a Worker in a Supporting Role, documentary: **Douglas Stillwell**, Carpenter and job assistant, RLS Memorial Grass House Project

For Best Performance as Leading Lady in a volunteer role: **Evelyn Wells**, Chairman, Wai'oli Committee, Salvation Army Women's Auxiliary.

For Best Performance as Leading Man in a volunteer role: **Malcolm Jackson**, Chairman, Wai'oli Advisory Committee, Salvation Army Advisory Board.

For Best Performance as a Volunteer in an unclassified series: **Jane Fujimoto**, 30 year volunteer at Wai'oli.

For Performances of Excellence in Volunteer roles, a continuing series: **Lib Speer**, **Lucille Mackin**, **Venona Honchell**, SA Women's Auxiliary members.

For Best Performance as an Artist in an Original Production: **Bill Cooper**, UH Professor and Wai'oli customer, for producing the life-sized rocking horse displayed at Wai'oli which sold for $5,000, half of which he donated to Wai'oli for making the sale.

For Best Performance as Patrons in a "Customery" role: **Charles** and **Barbara Hendricks**, valued customers, for their faithful patronage, always bringing guests, always making reservations and always paying their bill…

For Best Performance as a Leader in an Administrative Role: **Major Mervyn Morelock** – Hawaiian Islands Divisional Commander for his constant patronage and visible support of the Wai'oli Tea Room operation…

Most Inspirational Worker: **Elsie Monma**, Assistant Manager, 26 years continuous employment at The Wai'oli Tea Room.

For Best Performance as a Worker in a Supervisory Role: **Phyllis Kolo**, 10 year employee, head waitress, baker extraordinaire,

For Best Performance as a Worker in a Production Role: **Alden Kaleohano**, Head Cook, 2 year employee, Perfect Attendance.

For Best Performance as a Volunteer in a "Relative" role: **Dr. Robert Stillwell**, business advisor, counselor, consoler, listener, helper, etc., etc.

"TAKES THE CAKE" AWARD for Best Performance of motivated effort: **Sam VeraCruz**, five-year worker – Maintenance, kitchen and gardens…" The day he washed the manager's car…!"

It was a very special day and everyone enjoyed the spirit of appreciation.

A LIVE NATIVITY

*C*hristmas of 1983 was the inaugural performance of The Salvation Army's Live Nativity presented in the Memorial Garden fronting Waiʻoli Tea Room. Early in December producer, Clarence Ing, worked with Doug Stillwell in the building of appropriate fencing for the live animals that would be brought in for the five night pre-Christmas pageant. A scaffolding and stairs, wiring for the star, the stable and hay were all in place for what has become a traditional part of Christmas in Manoa Valley. Jan (Mrs. Gordon) Young was a key figure in its inception and continues to direct the production every year. Salvation Army church members, as well as men and women in Salvation Army treatment programs, volunteer to portray the Biblical characters each night.

"One night a few years ago, a young woman standing near me was telling her friend that ten years earlier she had been the "angel." According to Jan Young, she had been in one of the rehab programs at that time.

1998 was the 16th year that traffic patterns changed at the intersection of Manoa Road, Oahu and Lowrey Avenues, allowing hundreds of people to gather for the portrayal at thirty minute intervals on the nights preceding Christmas.

The first Live Nativity

1984

By January of 1984 the daily pressures of Wai'oli's economic survival were taking a toll on my energy. Business seemed excellent but it was never enough to pay all of the bills. The overhead and maintenance of acres of tropical gardens, constant repairs to old buildings, freezers and refrigerators that ran 24-hours a day, a minimal staff with very high employer costs for benefits, and the federal minimum wage law, 'though necessary, was more than the business could handle. Wai'oli wasn't alone in this plight. Similar problems were breaking-the-backs of small business, especially small restaurants, all over the Islands.

Following a doctor-ordered leave-of-absence, I left my active employment with The Salvation Army as manager of the Wai'oli Tea Room. It was a traumatic decision to make. Wai'oli was in my blood! I wanted so much to see it succeed!

10

THE NEXT FOUR YEARS

ew managers were hired over the next four years and each tried very hard to improve Wai'oli's financial situation. Every year the debt grew greater. The Salvation Army Women's Auxiliary of Honolulu had become an active force in Wai'oli's day-to-day operation, funding improvements from time to time, arranging flowers, and hostessing or helping in the gift shop. Major Mervyn L. Morelock, the Divisional Commander, was heard to say more than once, "Over my dead body will Wai'oli be closed!" He was a great supporter of the Tea Room and helped in every way possible. The Morelocks were transferred in June of 1986.

The 1987 announcement by The Salvation Army to close the Tea Room met with a resounding hew-and-cry from patrons, neighbors, and local citizens. "They can't do it, they said," "Wai'oli is part of the fabric of Honolulu's historic heritage!" Hundreds of people had been nurtured through The Salvation Army's Children's Home and ultimately, through the Wai'oli Tea Room with its vocational training. Some Auxiliary members offered monthly financial support. Individuals pledged their support by underwriting all of the expenses for one month. But it wasn't enough to sustain the on-going burden of the expensive operation. A disturbing discourse between Salvation Army officials and concerned citizens continued for many months. Finally, on orders from mainland officials, the Divisional Commander, then Major Bill D. Luttrell, closed the Wai'oli Tea Room in February of 1988.

Tears were shed and disappointed patrons were turned away over the ensuing months as they arrived at Wai'oli with great expectations. Subsidies from Salvation Army sources could no longer be justified when there were so many other real people needs within the Salvation Army's responsibility in Honolulu.

THE WAI'OLI CONFERENCE CENTER

AN ALTERNATIVE

*T*he Tea Room property was utilized for community meetings and seminars under the direction of long-time Advisory Board member, Steve Murin, who volunteered his time for more than two years. Bookings were made for small group meetings, seminars, or catered luncheons using the dining rooms and the kitchen. While consideration was being given to the Tea Room's future, this provided security as well as some income to help offset the maintenance costs. The whole property is so wide open, it was difficult to secure, but Murin's presence was known and provided

Steve Murin receives Recognition Award from Major Joe Noland upon his retirement from the Wai'oli Conference Center in 1992.

some degree of activity every day. Many out-buildings and storage areas were stacked with furnishings and equipment that current users did not wish to use. Major Bill Luttrell spoke highly of Murin's work and the responsibility he held during these troubled years. Steve Murin retired from this position in 1992.

New Administration 1990

Majors Bill and Gwen Luttrell were transferred from Honolulu in June, 1990, their successors being then-Majors Joe and Doris Noland. Divisional Secretary, Major Kurt Berger was second in command, and served as the conduit through which a good transition of leadership was made. With the day-to-day business of the organization the major part of Berger's responsibilities, the fate of the Wai'oli Tea Room appeared to be a constant headache to Salvation Army administration in Honolulu. Many members of the advisory board were aware of Wai'oli s financial state and were suggesting it be torn down and another use be found for the property. The buildings were nearing seventy years old. Reroofing and painting projects over the years were effecting "patchwork" improvements. Its rundown condition could no longer be hidden.

The Tea Room was being rented on a month-to-month basis to a local catering firm with an eye to reopening with a daily restaurant service. In November of 1990 the new tenant released a story to the *Honolulu Advertiser* which carried the announcement of plans for reopening. The Department of Land Use responded within the first hour of the release with the message:

> "More than one year has elapsed since the 1988 closing and you are without a valid Use Permit. A new Conditional Use Permit – Type II must be awarded before the Wai'oli Tea Room can reopen as a restaurant."

Dealings with the Tea Room's problems were further aggravated by the complexities and emotional trauma in the closure of The Army's Residential Treatment Facilities for Children and Youth; formerly the famous boys home established in the early Twenties on 22nd Avenue in the Kaimuki area. These major concerns must have weighed heavily on the new administration.

New Salvation Army personnel appeared to be developing a good understanding of what the Tea Room had been, the purpose it had served, and its present condition. As to its destiny, a quick decision was not anticipated. It was suggested by the Advisory Board that a proposal be drawn up looking at the bigger picture of the Wai'oli Tea Room; its place in the future of The Salvation Army in Honolulu. Should it be renovated again and, if so, for what purpose? Should the property be used for an activity more contemporary with the times? Who knew The Salvation Army, the property, and the Tea Room's history well enough to write a reasonable proposal?

I was contracted to develop this proposal, working with a committee who could implement recommendations for Salvation Army approval at the Territorial level. I was sure that Noland wanted to save Wai'oli if there were any possibility of its reclamation.

The Department of Land Use edict, following the November 1990 announcement to open for business, stated that a new Conditional Use Permit Type II must be awarded before food services could restart. This meant that the entire premises would have to be brought up to present day building codes. A grandfather clause had been in effect over many years and recent band-aid repairs would not hold up to a close building inspection. Noland pondered the situation with the Advisory Board and staff, many of whom were well acquainted with the property and its structural deficits. The original recommendation concerning Wai'oli's future was amended to include a draft outlining the extent of work needed relative to the awarding of a new Conditional Use Permit Type II.

I knew the Wai'oli property very well and what I didn't know, my son, Doug, did; such as the location of water valves and meters, gas lines, electrical junctions, grease traps and drains. Over the ensuing months Doug and I ran the gamut with plumbers, electrician's, carpenters, an arborist and landscapers. Building contractors produced plans and estimates for upgrading everything from water lines and meters to new power lines, including a new weather head power terminal on the roof. The application required a schematic drawing with a striping of the parking lot to show numbered spaces relative to the dining areas size and patron expectations. Over the previous ten years new Salvation Army offices and programs had been established on the property with a gradual infringement into the former Tea Room parking lot. This arrangement had been approved by the City, with permits being issued for that purpose. Now the plans required available parking relative to the square footage of the dining areas, and public restrooms had to be brought into ADA (American with Disabilities Act) standards.

Members of The Historic Hawaii Foundation were conducting a meeting at Wai'oli one day in the early stages of my work, and Paul Onishi, the current tenant, was in attendance. Following the meeting he shared the discussion with Noland emphasizing the thought that if the Wai'oli Tea Room were on the State Register of Historic Places it might influence the City's decision in awarding a new Use Permit. It wouldn't remove any building code requirements but it would strengthen the application, he had been told. So, while new work was in progress, I met with officials of the State Office on Historic Preservation and was given nomination papers to be completed and subsequently offered for election to the Register.

In-depth research took me into newspaper morgues, State archives and very old Salvation Army files. It would result in a lengthy document containing specific details of Wai'oli's historic significance, its architecture, architects names, and drawings of the property. With the support and endorsements of prestigious signatures, i.e., U.S. Senators and local elected officials, approval of The Salvation Army Territorial Headquarters in California, and The Salvation Army's Honolulu Advisory Board, the completed nomination was submitted. On June 28, 1991 Wai'oli Tea Room was elected to the State of Hawaii Register of Historic Places. This set the wheels in motion for the State's subsequent nomination of the Tea Room to the National Register.

As I began my serious surveying of the buildings and grounds, once again in pursuit of the new Use Permit, I came upon constant reminders of earlier years when the property was alive with activity; people working and people visiting. Traversing the walkways in the rear gardens I could almost smell the guava and mango cooking in the jelly house remembering days when hot sparkling tiny jars were positioned row after row on trays awaiting the pour of the jams and jellies that would fill them. Peering through age old windows dimmed by cobwebs, I could see the shelves empty now, with ghosts of unused tiny bottles spilled from weathered boxes under a table. Weathered, indeed; the old roof had broken through leaving a gaping whole for the daily rains to run their course. Adjacent storage rooms used to hold huge sacks of flour, sugar, and cornstarch. How well I remember the tedium of the monthly inventory process, counting every can and every sack in the dark old rooms. The gift shop storage room, originally a single car garage for the upstairs apartment, now held floor to ceiling shelves, probably twenty-foot high, filled with *tapa* covered boxes of all sizes, gift wrapping papers, Christmas ornaments and odd shaped decorations. I remember the day when Jerry Payne and Gil Frauenheim, dear (late) husbands of Beverly and Ele of the Women's Auxiliary, donned their carpenter aprons and built those sturdy shelves to help me get the room organized.

Recognizing the absolute need for change in Waiʻoli's future, I knew that if things went as planned all of this would be cleaned out soon and a new day would begin.

It was a ten-month journey toward a new Conditional Use Permit commencing in July of 1991. By April of 1992, the new Permit Type II was in hand; a single page letter accompanying a very thick package of important documentation.

RECONSTRUCTION BEGINS

With the new Use Permit in hand, work moved rapidly toward the rebuilding of the Tea Room. The Salvation Army in

Honolulu was in the throes of a capital campaign to raise $8 million dollars for new building projects throughout the division (State). For almost two years, a professional firm had been retained to develop preliminary campaign materials including local leadership for major gifts. J.W. A. "Doc" Buyers, CEO of C. Brewer & Co., served as General Campaign Chairman. He personally hosted many of the presentations that were made with firms and individuals. A sizeable base of pledges toward the campaign goal were in hand by December of 1991 as Noland deliberated over the campaign income received to-date. He proposed that a full-time campaign coordinator be hired to replace the professional firm by March of 1992.

Architect Lloyd Sueda & Associates, AIA, and contractors, SteelTech, Inc., were moving ahead with the reconstruction projects and once again, my contract work was nearing completion. I received a personal call from Major Noland asking if I would consider working with the Capital Campaign full-time. After some thought on the subject, I agreed, and with board approval of the hiring, I became the Capital Campaign Coordinator/Director. My office was situated in the small two room building adjacent to the Tea Room, built c. 1966 as the Tea Room manager's office. Capital campaign business took my full attention, but the office's close proximity to the Tea Room gave me ample opportunity to be aware of everything of any impact that was going on there, relative to the reconstruction.

The *Honolulu Advertiser* had carried the story of the Use Permit awarding, and plans for a reopening following meetings with the Neighborhood Board. Contracts had been signed with the architect and builders for the renovation. Worm-eaten walls, sills, and doorways were torn out and replaced with new materials accomplishing an end result as close to the original as was possible. A low roofed entry erected c. 1958 was replaced with a grand structure of six steel-supported stone columns identical in appearance to the seventy-year old columns fronting the adjacent lanai. By this time the lessee had begun to rev up his restaurant plans and within a short time we could dine on the lanai, albeit amid some dust and clutter of reconstruction

Finishing touches to the interior were ordered by interior decorators under the close supervision of the Divisional Commander, to assure the best presentation possible. This included wall coverings, paint finishes and colors, and the placement of framed photographs depicting Manoa Valley and this Salvation Army property in the Twenties.

The addition of an Executive Assistant to the Capital Campaign office provided a good balance of responsibilities. This attractive young woman possessed the necessary office skills and would be involved in the presentations with corporate executives and community leadership. Kanoe Cazimero had graduated from Kamehameha Schools before attending the University of Hawaii and had a good background in promoting special events. Over the next fourteen months we worked inseparably representing The Salvation Army every day in a different business setting. Kanoe was a strong force in the designing and coordinating of a major benefit set at the Wai'oli Tea Room in June of 1992, bringing together campaign principals, city officials, and Salvation Army dignitaries for the purpose of accelerating attention to the campaign and the need for capital funds.

On September 11, 1992, all Hawaii awoke to the eerie sounds of wailing sirens which exploded on a sleepy populace at 5:30 A.M. From the previous night's news commentary and weather reports, this was not a surprise announcement. Hurricane Iniki had changed its westerly course at 90 degrees and mounting gale winds were skirting Oahu's leeward coast creating near panic from Waikiki to Waianae. By noon she had blasted Oahu's northwest shore along the Waianae coast, and was moving in a direct path toward the south shore of the Island of Kauai. Telephone contact with my own family in Koloa, just inland from Poipu Beach, was cut off at 1:30 P.M., the recorded hour at which the hurricane hit its land target. For the next three hours 160 mph gale force winds and rain wreaked devastation throughout the small island's entire land mass, leaving thousands of residents and as many visitors without electricity, drinking water, and shelter. The small force of Salvation Army officers and volunteers on Kauai literally flew into action in preparation of relief efforts that profoundly affected many people whose lives had been torn apart in these few afternoon hours. By the next morning, backup personnel were arriving to assess the devastation and communicate emergency needs back to Oahu stations as people across America were anxious to aid in any way possible. This frightening storm would have a marked affect on The Salvation Army's capital campaign progress, compounding an already near recession economy. Where major gifts previously had been designated, many were redirected to hurricane relief; a worthy cause, indeed. Efforts to advance further fund-raising for anything but the hurricane relief would have proven pointless, whereupon the capital campaign was brought to a gradual conclusion. The Salvation Army was relying heavily on pledges that would come due over a five year period.

A grand celebration was staged the following May 1993, to bring closure to the capital campaign and at the same time, highlight The Salvation Army Centennial in Hawaii; 100 Years of Aloha. The program featured a tableau of important milestones throughout the 100 year history. A centennial poster by local artist, Lori Kilpatrick, was given to each guest as the evening concluded. The high-profile event contributed greatly to the positive image The Salvation Army held in Honolulu and in the State of Hawaii.

THE TEA ROOM REOPENS

After a five-year hiatus The Waiʻoli Tea Room's reopening in 1993 introduced a new and different format, again in a lease agreement. The formal lease was drawn up by local attorney, Carol M. Egan, Esq., a member of The Salvation Army Advisory Board of Honolulu. Paul Onishi, the lessee and part-owner of Tad & Pat Catering, was a

respected restaurateur who attracted a clientele from Honolulu society
and the University of Hawaii community for a new luncheon offering.
A buffet presentation was added and it was exciting to see the establishment in operation once again and the property being maintained to
show its great beauty. New lighting fixtures throughout enhanced the
sheen of new wall, sash, and door surfaces. Clean glass windows sparkled
against the valley's colorful backdrop. Patrons gathered on the new entry
lanai as seating was often slowed by throngs of patrons gathering again
for special celebrations or just a leisure lunchtime. Fresh flowers and pot-
ted trees filled the dining rooms open spaces. So close to my office, it
became my daily lunchroom shared often with family and friends. I was
so proud of the Army's courage and determined ability to bring Wai'oli
back to this place in time.

One of the most beautiful events held there immediately following
the restoration was a farewell banquet honoring then-Lt.Colonels Joe
and Doris Noland in November of 1993. The Tea Room business had
been growing and the event was like an open house with everyone
admiring its new appearance. The guest list included Frank and Joyce
Fasi, he the Mayor of Honolulu, Doc and Elsie Buyers, heads of corpo-
rations, advisory board members past and present, a table of former
employees, and a group of women who had grown up as children in the
girls home and at Wai'oli in the Twenties and Thirties and Forties. The
conversation noise-level during dinner was a real measure of the excitement that was in the air. It was a memorable evening.

Business continued through 1994 and into 1995, but Hawaii's economic downturn was being felt very much in small restaurants and
catering businesses. By the summer of 1995 the Tad & Pat Catering
lease was faltering and monthly obligations were delinquent month after
month. The Salvation Army recalled the lease at the end of the year.

11

A NEW WAIʻOLI TEA ROOM RISES

xclusive, Inc., had been good tenants of The Salvation Army
since the early Seventies, leasing the Waiʻoli Chapel for
their thriving wedding business. The rent was always paid on
time and they took excellent care of the property within the agreement
of the lease. They had watched with mixed emotions, I am sure, the
many changes in Waiʻoli's management over time. When the vacancy
became obvious numerous small businesses expressed interest in leasing
the Tea Room for their restaurant operations. The Walker family
who owned Exclusive Inc., expressed great interest in expanding their
lease to include the Tea Room and after lengthy negotiations with then
Divisional Commander Major Chris Buchanan, a new lease was
approved in 1997. The Walker family, headed earlier by Wesley Walker,
now retired, come from a background of Christian ministry. For many
years the family had lived in Japan where the senior Walker served as a
minister. Son Denny Walker is the business manager and his brother,
Gary Walker, an ordained minister, conducts most of the weddings that
take place in the Waiʻoli Chapel. With his wife, Rebecca, they are managing the Tea Room operation. Rebecca's touch is evident in everything
from the appearance of the gardens and placement of new furnishings
and floral décor, to the food presentations and delightful baked goods
with their distinctive new Waiʻoli Tea Room packaging.

The manicured grounds and buildings appear to be even more
beautiful today than in the past. The Salvation Army can be proud, once
again, of its ownership of the Waiʻoli Tea Room established on these
Manoa grounds in 1922.

*Photo of Waioli Tea Room
today. Exterior and Interior.*

Wai'oli Tea Room Historic Plaque Unveiling—March 3, 1998. Bette pictured with Commissioners Edwards, DCs Mowery, former DCs Morelock, Advisory Board Chair Phil Russell, and far left Rebecca Walker present Wai'oli Tea Room Manager.

In March of 1998 Major Don Mowery, Divisional Commander, approved a public announcement of the Wai'oli Tea Room's election to the State and National Registers of Historic Places. In formal ceremonies, Western Territorial Commander, Commissioner David Edwards removed a silk veil revealing the State of Hawaii Historic Site plaque that was permanently cemented onto one of the new stone pillars in Wai'oli s entry lanai. Funds for the purchase of the plaque were provided by the late Brigadier Sara Kennedy-Jones whose life-long career as a Salvation Army officer began at the Wai'oli Tea Room and The Salvation Army Children's Home in 1929. Sara came back to Wai'oli to celebrate her 91st birthday in December of 1997; her first return since leaving Hawaii in 1932. Brigadier Sara Jones died in Los Angeles, California in the Fall of 1998.

Rebbecca & Gary Walker

Throughout the little Tea Room's seventy-seven years on a glorious hillside drenched almost daily with sunshine and showers, rainbows continue to hold a promise; a reminder of God's goodness in all things where He is honored. Truly, the Wai'oli Tea Room has been an honoring of His word reflecting Proverbs 14:26 "His children shall have a place of refuge."

It is my dream and prayer that the Wai'oli Tea Room shall continue to thrive for generations to come. You, the reader of this brief history, can help to make it happen!

"Come back to Wai'oli!"

12

ADDENDA

BABY JULIA

1906–1912: The First Six Years at
The Salvation Army Children's Home in Honolulu

*I*t was 1908. I was two years old when my father, Joseph Pratae, brought my brother George and me to live in The Salvation Army "Rescue" Home on South King Street in Honolulu. My mother had died in childbirth and my Spanish father, a gardener by trade, was off to Alaska in search of gold. He had made friends with Clara Long, one of the home matrons, while arrangements were being made. Not knowing

Julia–second from right. George–second from left, back row.

just when he would return to Honolulu, he asked Clara if she personally would look after me. I was two-years old and quite ill at the time. Clara promised to "look after" me and moved me right into her own bedroom so that she could care for me at night.

It was from this start that a lifetime relationship was to develop and Clara Long would adopt me as her own daughter. From the first day, we were inseparable. In 1912 I moved with Clara Long and Libby McAbee to San Antonio, Texas, where they were appointed to do the same work they had done in Honolulu. Staff-Captain Libby McAbee took up guardianship of my brother, George, to keep us close together.

We all moved to Seattle eventually and attended the Seattle No. 1 Corps on Washington Street. Libby McAbee was the Aunt of a wonderful young man named Frank Richard McAbee, whom I married in 1926. We were married for 72 years. Dick passed away in 1999 at the age of 93.

Julia Pratae Long McAbee
April, 1999

LIZZIE REMEMBERS

Excerpted from a taped interview with Dr. Robert Stillwell when she came to Manoa for a visit in 1989. He took her on a tour of the grounds.

My family came from England to Boston where my mother was born. When she was 12 years old they journeyed to Hawaii around South America's Cape Horn, stopping in Louisiana and in San Francisco. My grandparents were Christian missionaries; my grandmother a nurse.

I was born in 1906 in Honolulu. We lived on Punahou Street. It must have been 1910; I was four years old. My parents were divorced and my mother and I were living with my grandparents. They all had to return to England on family business and I was put in the care of The Salvation Army Home while they were away. I thought they would be back in a few weeks.

I spent the next thirteen years in the Home and remember very much, even though I was only four years old at the outset.

On that day in 1910: We were greeted in the reception area of the building by the administrator, Staff-Captain Libby McAbee who was a friend of my grandmother. Miss McAbee welcomed me and took all of the papers from my grandmother. The separation from family made a

1908 Staff-Captain Libby McAbee and Commandant Clara Long with Baby Julia..

mark on my memory because I remember it as a terrible day in my life, being taken away from my mother. I was so frightened....I cried and cried for hours and they had to put me in a special room because of my screaming and kicking.

There was only one building on the grounds when I arrived and it was named "Wilcox Cottage" after the man who gave the money to have it built. George N. Wilcox was a very generous man, a son of missionaries to the Island of Kauai. He made his wealth from his engineering developments in the processing of sugar cane and The Salvation Army was always at the forefront of his giving to charity.

The building had a gorgeous lanai. The wood floors shone brightly. They used oil, no wax. Wicker rocking chairs were on the lanai but we could not sit there. The children were not allowed in the parlor or living room, either. There were beautiful ferns hanging in baskets all around the lanai. The entrance was off the lanai with full walls of glass. When I was older I lived in a dormitory-like room on the second floor with twenty or more girls on each side of the building. In easy access from second floor windows was a flat part of the roof. We would love to have crawled out there, but were forbidden to do so. Another section held cribs for the very small children and babies. We often took care of the babies. It was part of our education.

With so many children to care for, of course there were strict rules and a very structured schedule. We were awaken early every morning by a loud bell, and we made our own beds exactly as we were shown after brushing our teeth and doing our bathroom thing. A bath could be taken only once a week to conserve water. The Home had its own water system; watershed – catchment. I learned that the property was connected to the water department but it was seldom used. The water catchment sheds were on the steep hillside above the chapel and dormitory buildings. This was where we went to hide when we were running away from one of the teachers to worry her a little bit. We each had our own guava tree and put our own "mark" on it. This was a great memory!

We dressed ourselves for school with designated dresses; no shoes. We wore shoes only at Christmas time when we were dressed up, sometimes in costume for the annual Christmas performance. It's the only time I remember having shoes tied on me. We wore white dresses. I loved Christmas. It was the greatest time. Everyone, parents and families, the Cookes, the Dillinghams, the Wilcoxes; all were invited to the Christmas program at the Children's Home. The assembly hall was full every time. All holidays were made special while I lived there: Easter, Thanksgiving, Halloween. We celebrated every holiday beautifully. It was a great place to live and I don't have any bad memories.

Well, maybe one: Miss Wolf was a teacher at the home and I did not like her at all. She was Russian and seemed very young to be an authority figure, which did not lend to her popularity with the older girls. She lived on our floor in the same building. When I was in my teens I can remember being sent to the Kaimuki (boys') Home as punishment for being "unruly." The Kaimuki buildings were started in 1916 and many of us were sent there from time to time to pick up stones and other debris around the grounds when we misbehaved.

The Children's Home chapel looked like a castle to me. It had sort of a tower in the middle. We attended Sunday School and went there for some classes during the week. We all went to Manoa School in the neighborhood."

Studying old photographs, Lizzie commented on her very straight hair and the assistance of two older girls, Georgia and Amelia, who took delight in picking-on her while braiding her hair so tightly she couldn't see, she said. "I didn't have "bangs." My hair went straight back."

"We didn't have much to do with the boys who were in the home at Kaimuki. Once in awhile we were together for special programs. But we couldn't even talk to the boys when we were all together. The rules were very strict, especially in this area.

As I grew older it seems most of my chores involved the laundry and hand ironing of table cloths and napkins. I was sixteen years old during the time of construction of the Wai'oli Tea Room. It was a very exciting time, a bit like watching your own new house being built and anticipating the day you would move in. I remember a very humid day in November, it was very warm and it rained off and on all through the day. The kitchen and dining rooms were beautiful and the Wai'oli Tea Room was going to be blessed with the attendance of very important guests who had provided the money and who were involved in its construction. I had been given three baskets of table linens to be ironed for the big dedication reception that was going to be on Saturday, three days away. My right arm was becoming muscle-bound, lifting and moving a heavy clumsy iron for what seemed like hours and hours every day. The job was never really done! By the time one basket was empty another appeared in its place.

On Friday afternoon, I remember the agony of the last batch of big table cloths. My hair fell in my face as I labored over the narrow ironing board. It was so hot and I could hear my friends in the kitchen laughing as they were preparing all of the special fare that would be served at tomorrow's reception. I was praying that there would never again be a special reception day when I would have to do all of the ironing.

I finished just in time to head quickly to a band rehearsal. We were playing at the reception. I played the drum in the Girls Home Band, and I was good too. My teacher was a man who had been taught by John Philip Souza. Sometimes he swore at me in Hawaiian.

It was a bittersweet part of my life, most of which I think I hated at the time because I didn't know where my family was. But in later life I think of it as the best time of my growing up years. I had six sisters, but they were in Boston. After I left the Salvation Army home in Honolulu when I was seventeen (1923) I went to San Francisco to live with relatives there. After a short time I moved to Grants Pass, Oregon where I met my husband. We were married there and had ten children; 3 boys and 7 girls. He died in 1957; I was 51 years old. I'm now 83 and live in San Francisco. I have 55 grandchildren and about 40 great grandchildren."

EVA KALAUANA

EVA KALAUANA lived at the Girls' Home and worked at the Wai'oli Tea Room during the years from 1923 to 1940.

*orn in 1913, Eva is a tiny woman of Hawaiian, Chinese, Dutch and English descent. She was born in Queen's Hospital in Honolulu and says she is related to Queen Liliuokalani. When her parents divorced, she was given to The Salvation Army Children's Home in Manoa Valley, c. 1923, until arrangements could be made for her care elsewhere. When her mother remarried (a naval officer, Jackson) she went to live with them. The details of her returning to the Children's

(left) Jane Libby and Eva Kalauana (right).

Home are not clear, but she did indicate that her step-father, Jackson, loved her very much and wanted to adopt her legally. She was in the Home once again while she was a teenager and graduated from McKinley High School c. 1931. Reminiscing about her recollections of

Wai'oli Tea Room in the Twenties, she remembers Adjutant Harry Stillwell who taught brass instruments and directed bands at The Boys' Home and The Girls' Home. One of her best friends was Marjorie Stillwell who had an older brother, Harry. They both went to Punahou School.

Eva has lived her life physically challenged with a speech impediment. Verbal communication is difficult, although she moves in and out of conversations freely. Eva told of several jobs she had after she left high school; one which kept her living at the Girls' Home and working at Wai'oli Tea Room in the Twenties and Thirties. It was through this activity that she met Dr. Rod West and, subsequently, Dr. John Devereux, both of whom were members of The Salvation Army Advisory Board of Honolulu. The Board met monthly with lunch at the Wai'oli Tea Room, giving Eva opportunity to become recognized by many of Honolulu's prominent personalities.

In 1940 Eva Kalauana was invited to work for the Devereux family in their Manoa Valley home, housekeeping and caring for the four Devereux children. Dr. Devereux was a member of the Hawaii State Legislature, a position filled and held by his wife, Dorothy, for many years after his death.

Eva took great delight in showing us through her little home, provided for her by the Devereux family, just steps away from their property. In her living room is a makeshift bed on the floor where she says she sleeps more comfortably than in good beds in either of the two bedrooms. Her tiny dog, Nikki, keeps her company. Walls throughout the house hold framed art work and photographs of her family and the Devereux family. She is proud of her carved (probably Teak wood) chest which was a gift from her mother. She pointed out a beautifully carved koa table lamp that was a Devereux gift; a workman in the house stole it's companion piece leaving her with just the one. Stuffed animals sit attentively everywhere, ranging in size from four feet to a tiny elephant cuddled in the arms of its mother elephant; her favorite animal.

Jane Libby and Eva have become very good friends, especially since Dorothy Devereux's death in 1995. Lasting friendships were made and many lessons learned as she was growing up during her years in the Girls' Home. "Her respect and admiration of The Salvation Army has remained constant as she grows older," affirmed Jane Libby, who was helping to interpret her words during our visit in November, 1998. Jane explained that on every visit she is always presented with something to take home with her, be it a package of Oreo cookies or a bag of lemons from her own backyard tree.

DODIE COSCA

Dodie Cosca was seven years old in 1923…she remembers the day! Adapted from written text by Dodie's husband of nearly 40 years, John Germaine, of Honolulu.

Dolores Cosca Germaine

DOLORES COSCA, born April 12, 1916, was the second child born to young parents from the Philippines who had come to Hawaii seeking a new life. They worked hard on sugar cane plantations on the Island of Kauai. Dolores's older brother was given for adoption to a non-child-bearing couple in the camp. A younger sister, Irma, was born when Dolores was three years old and little sister, Mary, arrived two years later. All were baptized in the Roman Catholic church and had godparents. "Throughout our first years we traveled from camp to camp, harvesting the cane fields. We always returned to our small plantation home in Lihue. We had a loving family life, but tragedy struck us when my mother became severely ill with beriberi disease which I learned is a vitamin (thiamin) deficiency. She died and is buried in Hanamaulu, Kauai. My father worked conscientiously to keep us clothed and fed. We were attended by nearby family women.

Somehow the Kauai courts learned that we were without parental care and investigated our case. Our younger sister, Mary, was adopted by godparents, but Irma and I were sent to the Salvation Army children's home on Oahu. We all were in shock! My father threatened to kill himself, but it made no difference. In those days the courts were the 'final word' and we lost our pleas to stay with our father. It was such a sad day. We had become orphans. I will never forget the day when a lady from the courts took us to the Ahukini Harbor in Lihue. It was January 6, 1923 at 6 A.M. Irma and I had to be restrained, which only made us more unhappy. Daddy was on his knees crying as we boarded the steamship *"Waialeale"* for Honolulu. The ship's horn sounded and we sailed off. We were exhausted when we arrived in Honolulu Harbor at 7 A.M. January 7, 1923.

We were taken directly to the Salvation Army Girls' Home in upper Manoa Valley. Captain Jeanette Hodgen met us and signed documents to release us from the court escort. Captain Hodgen tried her best to comfort us and make us feel welcome. We went to the infirmary first for a physical examination. Next we were given proper clothing. We couldn't help but notice that everything around us was so clean. We were escorted by an older girl to bathe and get ready for breakfast. It was so different from anything we had ever seen, but at least we had each other. The daily routine was strictly scheduled and there were many rules. We met many more officers, those who were really "in charge," Major Carrie Sabine and Commandant Rachel Payne. They seemed very friendly.

Over time we became familiar with the whole campus. The dormitory buildings were called "cottages." The property abutted the Cooke Estate on one side; about seven acres in all. The farm area had barns for livestock (cows and chickens). Upper Manoa road was a single lane driveway separating the campus from the farm. The land and funds for the construction of all the buildings on the property had come from wealthy landowners. The 13 buildings were:

- **Dillingham Cottage** was for infants to age six girls.
- **Cooke Cottage** was for girls age seven to 10 years.
- **Main building** housed the teen-aged girls and served as the main dining facility, shower room, clothing storage and dormitory.
- **Wilcox Cottage** was also for teen-agers with additional space for older working girls, most of whom worked at the Wai'oli Tea Room.
- **Kamakana Cottage** was the headquarters, officer's residence, and business office.
- **Cooke Assembly Hall** was our church building. We had a
- **Playhouse building**
- **Laundry building**
- **Gymnasium**
- **Infirmary**
- **Caretaker's Home**
- **Barns** for the cows and chickens, and
- The **Wai'oli Tea Room**

Soon after our arrival we started school at the Manoa Elementary School, not far from the Home. Our daily regimen included specified study hours to do our homework. We walked to school unless Mr. Chun drove us there. He was the only man around the Home. He served in many capacities: gardener, farmer, driver, utilityman and related duties. He was a very helpful person and cared about the girls as if they were his own family. Sundays were dedicated to prayer and church services. We all participated and were required to memorize verses from the Bible. This instilled in us a better understanding of the Bible and The Salvation Army's fundamental teachings.

1920 Laundry Building

There may have been times when our behavior deemed punishment. We were never spanked or whipped, but we were confined for periods of time, depending on the extent of our actions. It was humiliating so we were very careful to obey all the rules.

Major Carrie Sabine and Commandant Rachel Payne remained in administration until their retirement in 1928. Upon their subsequent deaths, a special plot in the Makiki Cemetery was donated by the Lucy Ward Estate and to date there are six marked stones; two officers and four children from the Home. My first husband was related to Lucy Ward.

As we grew older our responsibilities were increased. We supervised the younger girls. Our daily bathing consisted of a hot water tub bath with brown soap and lysol. Next we went to the warm showers and a final towel rub by an older girl. This was done for the younger girls up to age ten. We were also inspected for head lice, with fine tooth combing.

I went to Washington Middle School, then on to McKinley High School and graduation in 1936. I eventually moved into the upper teens dorm and later, was moved into the officers' quarters with Adjutant Dorothy Harris and her daughter, Norma. She was a nurse and due to my period of poor health, she insisted I move in with them. I went back to the Main Building with the senior girls as soon as I was stronger. I must admit that some of the senior girls were clannish and kept to themselves. As a whole, however, the girls got along well with each other.

Eva Liu was a very special staff person. She was the secretary and treasurer for the Girls' Home and the Salvation Army headquarters. She taught us financial matters, how to save and spend our meager allowance wisely. She was a very good friend to me and often counseled me on matters pertaining to womanhood. She was so admired for her compassion and honesty.

The saddest times of my life at the Home were "visiting days" which were the first and second Sundays of each month. Parents and relatives visited the girls who still had some attachment to their families. My sister and I had one visit from our father during the first six months after leaving Kauai. After a very pleasant day with him, time was up and he had to leave. This was another tearful time for us. After this visit, we never saw our father again. Subsequent Sunday visits about sixty percent of the girls would have visitors while the others sat on an over-looking hillside and watched, longing for a visit from our own families. After the visitors left, the lucky girls would come to us and share their gifts of candy and food. This was a time when we really became attached to each other. We were actually bonding as a family.

The Salvation Army Regimental All-Girls Band was famous island-wide. We played good music. The band mistress was Hana Hohoka. There were some thirty members when we joined at ages eleven and thirteen. I played French horn and baritone horn, and Irma played the bass horn. Our dear friend Lena played the cornet. One of our first male officers and leader was Captain George Johnstone. After learning, we graduated to the Main Band led by Adjutant Harry B. Stillwell or Divisional Commander, Brigadier Baynton. We played at the Salvation Army church on Beretania Street (between Fort Street Mall and Bethel Street). We played at the Oahu Prison on holidays: Mothers' Day, Easter, Thanksgiving, and Christmas. We played in the Kamehameha Day Parade, and our biggest treat was playing alongside the Royal Hawaiian Band at the Matson pier to greet tourists inbound on cruise ships. We played at the opening of Haleiwa Beach Park and at military bases on Oahu. We played and marched from Thomas Square to the center of town. We played at street corners during the Christmas holidays.

Over the years my younger sister, Mary, ended up in the Philippines. Prior to the Japanese invasion of the Philippine Islands, I took most of my savings and paid for her transport to Honolulu. She was old enough to travel by herself. I got her into the Home and a job at Waiʻoli Tea Room. Most of the teenagers at the Home worked at Waiʻoli Tea Room, learning to bake, and all of the related jobs in the kitchen. I worked at Waiʻoli from age 14 to age 24. I still remained in residence at the Home after I graduated from high school and went to the Honolulu Business College. Waiʻoli Tea Room was an excellent training base for all of the girls who participated in culinary arts. Miss Bertha Harshbarger was the operations manager. Ysabel Mullaney became a remarkable teacher with more than 50 girls a week in her cooking classes. Majors Iver and Laurina Torgerson were involved closely with The Tea Room in the late Thirties and their leadership and love was a strong factor in our developing years. Their daughter, Elnora (McIntyre) and I were close friends. Adjutant Harry Stillwell (Sr.), was a patient music instructor, and bandmaster of the Girls' Home Band. Captain George Johnstone (Sr.) took his place as bandmaster when the Stillwells left Hawaii in 1929 or 1930. Brigadier Albert Baynton, also a very qualified musician, was the bandleader in the 1931 picture.

Memorable visitors to the Tea Room included Admiral Halsey who loved our bakery's white bread. He came everyday to make this purchase and when he couldn't come himself, he sent his driver. On one occasion our supply had run out. This must have disturbed him a lot because after that he never came back. Helen Keller was introduced to me and her companion explained that by holding her hand she could communicate. She was deaf and mute, you know, a remarkable woman.

I was married to LeGros on October 15, 1941, in the first big wedding ceremony performed in the new Children's Chapel, built there in 1939. Major Erma Garman officiated.

Through many years girls and some staff from the Home have stayed in touch with each other, although many have died along the way."

Now in 1999, Dolores and her husband John Germaine attend services of The Salvation Army and often follow this with Sunday lunch at the Wai'oli Tea Room. They shared their table oneday with Bob and Bette Stillwell, for a time of reflection that resulted in her story being told.

ELSIE MONMA

A Wai'oli Fixture Retires After 32 Years

A RETIREMENT TRIBUTE by Bette M. Stillwell, presented at The Salvation Army Advisory Board of Honolulu, Annual Meeting May 12, 1989 • Ala Moana Hotel

Honolulu and all of Hawaii have been touched by the spirit of the Wai'oli Tea Room. Many memories began on the lanais or in the beautiful gardens of her noble girth. Wai'oli is filled with legends, many of whom are people...like

- Robert Louis Stevenson and the Princess Ka'iulani.

- Sabine and Payne (the founders of Wai'oli) who captured the intrigue of a little grass house.

- George N. Wilcox, Wai'oli's major benefactor

- Ann Leak, the famous woman who managed Wai'oli into its renowned luncheon business.

- Mercy Freitas who ran the kitchen and dining rooms with an "iron hand."

Elsie Monma

- Betty Poomaihealani, a memorable character in Wai'oli's colorful history.

- Miungo Lee Hall, a "Pillar" of Wai'oli.

- Jane Fujimoto, a faithful Wai'oli volunteer.

- Phyllis Kolo and Suk Cha Choe who stayed on and on, no matter who was the manager.

- Bette Stillwell, the "Renaissance" woman who had a dream for Wai'oli.

- Elsie Monma, a mirthful, spirited lady whose entire career was devoted to the Wai'oli Tea Room.

Elsie Monma joined the Wai'oli staff in 1957 during a time when important Salvation Army history in Honolulu was being enacted. Major Eric Newbould was the Divisional Commander and his administration started on the heels of a momentous period (c. Brigadier Bram Collier and Lt.Colonel William J. Parkins) when extremely valuable property had been sold off for the construction of new buildings on both the Kaimuki and the Wai'oli campuses. The old two-story "cottages" as they were called, were replaced with the sprawling one-floor buildings we recognize today in both locations.

It was during these changes that Wai'oli's kitchen and dining room classrooms were becoming separated from the children's programs as a major part of their training. Even in the Eighties, visitors to Wai'oli Tea Room remembered the days when there were children and young women of the Home working in the dining rooms and kitchen.

Elsie Monma began her Salvation Army and Wai'oli Tea Room education when, as the Gift Shop manager, she had to make frequent explanations trying to answer the constant questions about Wai'oli's origin, its roots, its people.

The Fifties may have been Wai'oli's "Hey-day"; the days when the cruise ships anchored regularly at Aloha Tower and all tours included the famous chicken luncheon at Wai'oli Tea Room. In these days the staff of local women scurried through the busy dining rooms serving as many as 300 covers in one day, I have heard. The singing of grace, the doxology, in Hawaiian was a traditional occurrence sending harmonic strains throughout the property every day around noon. An often heard question…."Why don't they sing anymore?" Elsie provided several answers, the best one being the fact that the current staff can't sing, or they're not Hawaiian, or they don't know the words. As Wai'oli's manager for more than five years one of my major function was the fielding of questions from so many return visitors and local guests. Elsie was a constant source of information.

Elsie was the gift shop manager. In the last ten years she was promoted to assistant manager, being the senior staff member and one who could function in every position. I cannot remember Elsie ever being absent from work. She was always on-time; a totally reliable worker; a constant personality; she never complained; she never "talk stink" about anyone or anything. When Elsie was on duty there was nothing to worry about. "Remember the awkward days during the renaissance, Elsie, when we had to move the gift shop into the Kauai Room for a little while, and the day "the rains came" when the roof was off – waterfalls everywhere?"

Buildings, programs and people are not forever. But Elsie Monma has given us an excuse to be reminded, if only briefly, of a wonderful memory that we will keep forever. Unforgettable Wai'oli!

Elsie Monma is Wai'oli personified; her soft warm glow, her grace and presence, a meek strength, her depth of being, her soul and treasure of history....

"Thank you Elsie Monma."

HE WENT ABOUT DOING GOOD

A Tribute to the Late Mr. George N. Wilcox of Kauai, Hawaii
By Commandant Rachel Payne (Retired)
Salvation Army Girls' Home - Honolulu Hawaii • January 26, 1933.

"They are gathering homeward from every land, one by one,
As their weary feet touch the shining strand, one by one,
Their brows are enclosed in a golden crown,
Their travel-stained garments are all laid down,
And clothed in white raiment, they rest on the mead,
Where the Lamb loveth His chosen to lead, one by one, one by one."

Mr. George N. Wilcox was called from his island home to higher service on January 21, 1933.

"*H*e is our friend who loved more than admired us, and would aid us in our great work." The Salvation Army has many friends in its great organization, friends in lands near and far, friends in all walks of life, and among all classes and conditions of mankind, friends from among the rich and poor, the learned and ignorant, friends among the outcasts of society and the downtrodden of earth, friends from the noble

rank and file of presidents and kings, and
last, but not least, a whole multitude of
friends from among the little children of the
world. Friends they are, the best and fairest
treasures of earth, for no man is useless
while he has a friend, no matter how far
down the social ladder he may fall; the outstretched helping hand of a friend will
impart new life and courage to the most
dejected, hopeless wreck of humanity.
"A friend," said a little waif of the street,
"is a person who knows all about a feller,
but loves him just the same"; and The
Salvation Army is rich in its wealth of sincere, devoted, and sympathetic friends. We
may submit to our reports giving creditable
accounts of much work accomplished,
buildings erected, or remarkable success,
and world-wide advancement, but, without
our good friends to aid us in our gigantic

task of seeking to serve and to save, much of the efforts of our grand old
Salvation Army would come to naught, without the financial assistance
and loyal devotion of its splendid host of friends. It is a true saying, we
can never replace a friend, we can and do replace other things in life, but
when we lose a friend, there is no substitute.

SUFFERED A GREAT LOSS

Within the last two years The Salvation Army in Hawaii and elsewhere
has suffered a great loss with the passing of many of its influential
friends. So many brave, noble souls have faithfully stood with us from
the days of The Army's infancy, with all the accompanying persecutions,
misunderstandings and difficulties that mark a new beginning. These

staunch supporters have generously and cheerfully given their time, money, and influence in the interest of our work, and, while we cherish their memories, we also grieve their loss.

Another call has come, another friend has joined the homeland circle. Early in the morning of Saturday, January 21, 1933, George Norton Wilcox, one of The Army's best and devoted friends, slipped peacefully away from the little "Islands of the Sea," to the fair Land of "Eternal Summer." The quiet passing of this most distinguished friend left a profound silence upon our hearts and minds, that eloquently expressed the pain of parting, that surpassed even the pathos of words or tears when the young people of The Salvation Army Boys' Home were told their good benefactor would not call to visit them again. Each boyish head bowed in silent reverence out of respect for the kindhearted, quiet man who had so generously provided a home for them; he was a friend to little children, and they loved him, too. Perhaps it was the influence of his kindly, gentle spirit that made such a deep impression upon their childish hearts. The girls and boys of The Army Institutions in Hawaii have lost one of the best friends they will ever have, for they were especially privileged in having a friend who was personally interested in their every welfare. He went about doing good like the Master he served. His deeds of loving service were not accompanied with the blowing of trumpets; his generous bestowal of gifts were distributed with quiet dignity and grace.

SUPREME JOY IN LIFE

The writer remembers on one occasion when requesting funds for the erection of the famous Waioli Tea Room, named by the donor himself, when the sum total amounted to many thousands, it was given in a gracious, modest manner, and he was not quite satisfied until he was assured the amount given would be sufficient to make the building complete in every detail. I have often marveled at his generosity, and how liberally he gave. No matter how often you presented some great need, you were always certain of a prompt response to your appeal. His giving was always accompanied with a merry little twinkle in his wonderful dark eyes, and a happy chuckle that came from a pure, unselfish heart, whose supreme joy in life was found in carrying others' burdens and making people happy. He was a master artist in the bestowal of gifts. One of the best pictures I have seen of the good friend of the poor is hanging on the walls of my memory over fifteen years of yesterdays, with Major Carrie Sabine, who was in command of the Girls' Home in Manoa Valley, and two other friends. We were sitting on the lanai of the main building of the Tea Room. Mr. Wilcox had called that day on important business connected with our work. The earnestness with which he made inquiries concerning the children's welfare made a deep impression upon my heart that time will never erase. He sat opposite my chair, holding in his hand a little plain straw hat that had mellowed in the sun of many summers, his leg crossed in true man fashion, which showed the top of his sock, neatly darned, the work of his own hands. Any woman might have been justly proud to execute such skill with needle and thread. It was a beautiful picture of a great man, whose unselfish life was so devoted in the interests of other people's comfort that he was entirely unmindful of his own. This old world is sadly in need of such rare souls like his, and while I am trying to write this unworthy tribute to our dear, departed friend my own heart has special reason for grateful remembrance.

HE LIVED FOR OTHERS

Major Sabine and I farewelled from the Manoa Valley Home six years ago, following the date of our retirement, where we had given many years of service among the children. It was through his appreciation of our feeble effort that we were given the home in which we live today. (The large stone house up the hill from the Tea Room back garden - 2501C Rainbow Drive) It is a gift of his gracious thoughtfulness, and every time I look through the window of my room the very stones from which it is built remind me of the solidity of his sterling character and the wholesome simplicity of his generous spirit. We have lost a friend, this gentle man of noble deed will not pass this way again; the influence of his noble life will forever remain. He lived for others. "It is a good thing to be rich, and a good thing to be strong, but it is a better thing to be beloved of many friends." As we journey together over life's troubled sea, friends of mine, let us strive to help make this world a better place in which to live. The words of the beautiful little prayer written by some unknown poet who was too modest to even sign his name, gives to us a very simple but Christlike attitude of true worship, for even Christ pleased not Himself.

> "Lord, help me to live from day to day,
> That even when I kneel to pray
> My prayer shall be for others.
> And when my work on earth is done,
> And my new work in Heaven begun,
> May I forget no crown I've won
> While thinking still of others."

13

WAIʻOLI TEA ROOM SONGS

WAIʻOLI TEA ROOM

© By Irmgard Farden Aluli
Performed at the Waiʻoli Renaissance, September 1981

Hele mai ʻoe (me aʻu)   Come with me to Waiʻoli
 ʻI Waiʻoli (Waiʻoli)
Ma ke awawa o Manoa   In Manoa
Nani uluwehi (nani uluwehi) Beautiful lush green valley
Mai e ai (ka mea ai)   Come to eat
 Inu liʻI liʻI (unu I ke ki) And sip a little tea
Hele mai, hel mai e na hoa! Come, Come friends!

Ona ka mea ai (ka mea ai) You'll enjoy good food
 Ono hoʻI (ka mea ai momona) And good desserts.
Ae, he wahi, he wahi ʻolu ʻolu Yes, in a most friendly hospitable
 Ae, ka hale inu ki Waiʻoli place, Waiʻoli Tea Room

"SWEET WAIʻOLI"

Words and music by Doris Noland, Honolulu 1993
Used as theme song by "Waiʻoli:" A Salvation Army vocal/string ensemble;
Clarence Orion, Al Orion, Lawrence Orion, Sam Abella, Jim Kobashigawa

In the Valley of Manoa, lies the sweet Waiʻoli garden,
Sweet Waiʻoli, singing waters, next to Heaven near my heart.
If you listen you will hear it, angels singing in the garden,
Sweet Waiʻoli, singing waters, songs of Heaven to my heart.
Song of blessing and forgiveness, songs of healing making whole,
Coming from the Living Waters, so refreshing to my soul.
If you listen you will hear it, angels singing in the garden,
Sweet Waiʻoli, singing waters, songs of Heaven to my heart.

Wai'oli Tea Room

©By Nancy Gustafsson
(Mrs. Victor Rittenband)

Up in the valley called Manoa
On the Island, O'ahu
Ko'ala anuhea ka'u I honi a'ku.

Wai'oli Tea Room, cool and peaceful
Magic rainbows–sparkling dew
Your lovely garden, bright and cheerful,
These memories I share with you.

Your fragrant flowers, sudden showers,
Then a sky, violet blue
Ko'ala anuhea ka'u I honi a'ku.

The little church there, filled with legends
Many people passing through
Ko'ala anuhea ka'u I honi a'ku.

There's a host of happy daughters remembering you,
Ko'ala anuhea ka'u I honi a'ku.

"MANOA"

By Kristian M. Fristrup 1934

In the ever blooming valley of Manoa
I have found a little, pretty heavenly paradise
Where the gleeful songbirds sing a sweet Aloha,
And the mountains lift the echo up to the skies.

Fairest Manoa, Oahu
You have so many charms that I can never forget;
Dearest Manoa, Honolulu
Your fragrant memories are lingering with me yet.

To this pleasant valley many malihini
Come to find refreshing comfort under the shady trees
While the voices of young kane and wahine,
Like a melody, come floating over the breeze.

When I gaze upon Manoa's perfect rainbow
With its gaily colored streamers spanning the skies above,
I remember all the happy hours you gave me
And I pledge again to you my tenderest love.

At Wai'oli Tea Room deep within Manoa
I would like to come and spend a season with you some day
In a corner by a table made of koa
I would love to while the time of twilight away.

Second Chorus
Come to Waioli,... ... Manoa
I would enjoy a cup of tea or coffee with you.
Come to Wai'oli in Manoa
There is a cozy little table reserved for two.

The song writer's daughter, Victoria Fristrup Martin and her husband Al Martin are long-time Manoa Valley residents.

ROSTER OF ADMINISTRATORS

DIVISIONAL COMMANDERS

The Salvation Army • Hawaiian Islands Division
Since start of Western Territory 1920

Date of Appointment	Rank • Name (at time of appointment)
May 1919	Brigadier Frank Waite
January 1921	Brigadier C. Wilfred Bourne
August 1924	Lieut.Colonel A. Merriweather
October 1926	Lieut.Colonel C.R. Boyd
October 1928	Brigadier Archibald Layman
October 1931	Brigadier Albert E. Baynton
November 1933	Brigadier James Bell
September 1938	Major Holland French
July 1941	Brigadier Arthur Brewer
September 1944	Major Adolf Kranz
September 1949	Brigadier H. Bramwell Collier
September 1956	Lieut.Colonel William J. Parkins
September 1957	Lieut.Colonel Eric Newbould
April 1962	Major Virgil Cline
June 1966	Brigadier Frank Moss
October 1969	Major Raymond Dexter
September 1973	Major Glenn E. Austin
September 1979	Major Kenneth Hood
November 1981	Major Mervyn Morelock
July 1986	Major Bill D. Luttrell
June 1990	Major Joe Noland
November 1993	Major Chris Buchanan
July 1997	Major Don Mowery

Children's Home Administration

Which included Waiʻoli Tea Room management:
Tea Room Built and opened in 1922

- Major Carrie Sabine
- Commandant Rachel Payne
- Major Carolyn Antrim
- Captain Dorothy Harris
- Majors Iver and Laurina Torgerson
- Major Erma Garman
- Adjutant Cecil Day
- Adjutant Don Pitt
- Captain Muriel Mitchell (Collier)

Waiʻoli Tea Room Managers

Following separation from the Salvation Army Children's Home
Administration... to Divisional Headquarters supervision in 1950

1947-1962	Ann Leak
1962-1966	Captain Hope Guernsey
1966-1968	Harley Baines (Lease)
1968-1971	Leo Qualls (Lease)
1971-1978	Miungo Lee Hall
1978-1984	Bette M. Stillwell
1984-1986	Kenneth Crawford
1986-1988	Anna Correa
1988-1992	Steven Murin–Waiʻoli Conference Center
1993-1996	Paul Onishi (Tad & Pat Catering) (Lease)
1997-Present	Gary & Rebecca Walker of Exclusive, Inc. (Lease)

*The Salvation Army (a California Corporation) is the owner of the
property, buildings, and programs operated on the grounds at 2950
Manoa Road, Honolulu HI 96822.*

Contributors & Resources

Original photos and letters from F. Richard McAbee

Personal letters of Sara Kennedy Jones

Personal letters and stories from Muriel Mitchell Collier

Personal interviews with Lizzie Gomes, Eva Kalauana and Dolores Cosca Germaine

Family Records of John Germaine

Letters of information from:

Carrie M. Doughty–Mystic Connecticut

Eric Newbould, former Divisional Commander

Kenneth Crusberg, Adolf Kranz, son-in-law

Minniebelle Shennan, former administrator of SA Children's Home

Colonel Henry Koerner, former staff officer

Archive files:

Grove Farm Plantation–Lihue, Kauai

The Salvation Army Divisional Headquarters

The Salvation Army Children's Home

The Wai'oli Tea Room

Salvation Army Disposition of Forces:

Hawaiian Islands Division 1896–1956

The War Cry, Salvation Army publication

Personal files of Bette Stillwell

Resources

Manoa – The Story of a Valley, Manoa Residents, 1994
   Mutual Publishing, Honolulu, Hawaii

Manual of Flowering Plants of Hawaii Warren L. Wagner, Derral R.
   Herbst, S.H. Sohmer. U.H. Press, 1990 Bishop Museum Press

In Gardens of Hawaii, Marie C. Neal, 1965 Bishop Museum Press

The Bishop Museum Archives, L.E. Edgeworth Photos

INDEX